Copyright

Low-Carb, High Protein Cookbook.
All rights reserved.

No part of this book may be reproduced, distributed, or transmitted in any form or by any means, including photocopying, recording, or other electronic or mechanical methods, without the prior written permission of the publisher, except in the case of brief quotations embodied in critical reviews and certain other non-commercial uses permitted by copyright law.

The content, recipes, and images in Low-Carb, High Protein Cookbook are the intellectual property of the author and are protected by copyright and other applicable intellectual property laws. Unauthorized use, reproduction, or distribution of any part of this book, in any format, is strictly prohibited and may result in legal action being taken.

This book is provided "as is," without warranty of any kind, express or implied, including but not limited to the warranties of merchantability, fitness for a particular purpose, or non-infringement. The author and publisher disclaim any and all liability for damages of any kind arising from the use of this book, including but not limited to indirect, incidental, or consequential damages.

Disclaimer

The information and recipes provided in Low-Carb, High Protein Cookbook are intended solely for informational and inspirational purposes. The content in this book is not a substitute for professional medical advice, diagnosis, or treatment, and should not be considered as such. While the recipes and dietary recommendations are crafted to support a healthy lifestyle, they are not tailored to meet specific medical needs or dietary requirements of any individual.

We strongly encourage you to consult with a healthcare professional, registered dietitian, or nutritionist before making any significant changes to your diet, especially if you have existing health conditions, dietary restrictions, or are on medication. Every person's nutritional needs and health situations are unique, and it is crucial to seek personalized guidance from a qualified professional to ensure that any dietary adjustments align with your health goals and medical history.

Please be aware that certain ingredients used in the recipes, such as nuts, dairy, gluten, or spices, may cause allergies or intolerances in some individuals. Always check the ingredients and nutritional content of the recipes, and adjust or omit them as needed to suit your personal dietary needs and preferences. If you experience any adverse reactions, discontinue the use of that recipe and seek medical attention immediately.

The author, publisher, and any contributors of Low-Carb, High Protein Cookbook are not responsible or liable for any health-related issues or complications that may arise from the use of the recipes or recommendations in this book. All users of this book assume full responsibility for their dietary and lifestyle choices. Additionally, the information contained in this book may not be complete, accurate, or up-to-date in light of new research and developments in nutrition and health. As such, we advise you to keep informed and consult reliable sources for the latest guidance.

By using Low-Carb, High Protein Cookbook, you acknowledge and agree that you are doing so at your own risk. The author and publisher disclaim all liability for any potential damage, injury, or loss incurred directly or indirectly from the use or misuse of the content and recipes provided in this book. Always prioritize your health and well-being by seeking professional advice when necessary.

Table of Contents

INTRODUCTION	01	Go through the Success Tips	16
		Monitor Your progress	16
CHAPTER 1: GETTING STARTED WITH	02	Make Recipes Work for You	17
LOW-CARB, HIGH-PROTEIN LIVING		Explore the index	17
Why Low-Carb, High-Protein?	04	Check the essential tools	17
Benefits of a Low-Carb, high-protein diet	08		
Helps in weight loss	08	**CHAPTER 2: BREAKFAST RECIPES**	
Better Regulation of Blood Sugar	09	1. Spinach and Egg Muffins	18
Encourages Physical Performance	09	2. Turkey and Avocado Breakfast Scramble	18
For older adults	09	3. Cheesy Omelet with Spinach and Mushrooms	19
Better Lipid Profile for Heart Health	10		19
Sustainability and Simplicity	10	4. Salmon and Avocado Breakfast Bowl	20
Who should not follow this diet?	10	5. Greek Yogurt and Almond Butter Parfait	20
Tips for Success	11	6. Sausage and Egg Breakfast Cups	21
1. Make a Weekly Meal Plan	11	7. Almond Flour Waffles	21
2. Track Your Intake	11	8. Bacon-Wrapped Asparagus	22
3. Celebrate your Small Victories	12	9. Zucchini and Cheese Hash Browns	22
4. Drink plenty of water	13	10. Chicken Breakfast Patties	23
5. Be creative and customize the meals	13	11. Coconut Flour Pancakes	23
6. Control Your Cravings	13	12. Mini Crustless Quiches	24
7. Incorporate exercise into routine	14	13. Keto Breakfast Burrito Bowl	24
8. Keep Low-Carb Essentials in Your Pantry	14	14. Low-Carb Breakfast Pizza	25
	14	15. Protein-Packed Veggie Omelet	25
Essential Ingredients and Tools	15	16. Chicken Breakfast Burrito	26
Protein sources	15	17. Peanut Butter Banana Oatmeal	26
Vegetables Low in Carbs	15	18. Greek Yogurt Power Bowl	27
Flavor enhancers	15	19. Sweet Potato and Egg Breakfast Hash	27
Low-carb sources for confectionary and desserts	16	20. Vegan Chocolate Protein Smoothie Bowl	28
Tools	16	21. High-Protein Pancakes	28
Tools for Meal Prep	16	22. Avocado Toast with Eggs	29
Cooking Utensils	16	23. Chia Pudding with Protein Boost	29
How to use this cookbook	16	24. Tofu Scramble with Vegetables	30
Begin with the introduction	16	25. Spinach and Feta Omelet	30

Table of Contents

CHAPTER 3: SNACK RECIPES — 31
1. Greek Yogurt Parfait with Berries and Nuts — 32
2. Hard-Boiled Eggs with Avocado Slices — 32
3. Protein-Packed Smoothie — 33
4. Veggie sticks with Hummus — 33
5. Cottage Cheese and Pineapple Bowl — 34
6. Rice Cakes with Almond Butter and Banana — 34
7. Tuna Salad with Crackers — 35
8. Apple Slices with Peanut Butter — 35
9. Vegan Energy Balls — 36
10. Trail Mix — 36
11. Cucumber and Hummus Bites — 37
12. Roasted Chickpeas — 37
13. Zucchini Chips with Parmesan — 38
14. Turkey and Guacamole Bites — 38
15. Baked Parmesan Crisps — 39

CHAPTER 4: LUNCH RECIPES — 40
1. Chicken and Spinach Stuffed Bell Peppers — 41
2. Salmon and Avocado Lettuce Wrap — 41
3. Eggplant and Chicken Caprese Bake — 42
4. Tuna and Cucumber Boats — 42
5. Shrimp and Cauliflower Rice Bowl — 43
6. Grilled Chicken and Asparagus — 43
7. Seared Tofu with Broccoli — 44
8. Garlic and Rosemary Roasted Chicken Thighs — 44
9. Beef and Bell Pepper Skewers — 45
10. Turmeric and Ginger Shrimp Stir-Fry — 45
11. Ginger Soy Salmon — 46
12. Balsamic Vinegar-Glazed Chicken Drumsticks — 46
13. Herb-Infused Lamb Meatballs — 47
14. Grilled Chicken and Quinoa Bowl — 47
15. Vegan Lentil Salad — 48
16. Turkey and Avocado Wrap — 48
17. Shrimp Stir-Fry — 49
18. Grilled Salmon Salad — 49
19. Vegan Chickpea Curry — 50
20. Chicken and Sweet Potato Bowl — 50
21. Vegan Buddha Bowl — 51
22. Turkey Meatballs and Zoodles — 51
23. Quinoa Stuffed Bell Peppers — 52
24. Lentil and Kale Soup — 52
25. Chicken and Chickpea Salad — 53

CHAPTER 5: SOUPS AND STEWS — 54
1. Chicken Zoodle Soup — 55
2. Beef and Mushroom Stew — 55
3. Spicy Shrimp Coconut Soup — 56
4. Turkey and Spinach Soup — 56
5. Creamy Cauliflower and Chicken Soup — 57
6. Egg Drop Soup with Spinach — 57
7. Beef Bone Broth Soup — 58
8. Kale and Sausage Stew — 58
9. Lemon and Dill Chicken Soup — 59
10. Creamy Broccoli and Cheddar Soup — 59

CHAPTER 6: DINNER RECIPES — 60
1. Mediterranean Baked Sardines — 61
2. Spicy Grilled Tuna Steak — 61
3. Teriyaki Sauce-Glazed Chicken Breast — 62
4. Garlic Butter Shrimp and Zoodles — 62
5. Beef and Vegetable Stir-Fry — 63
6. Pesto chicken with Roasted Brussels Sprouts — 63

Table of Contents

7. Cajun Salmon with Cabbage Slaw	64
8. Asian style Beef Lettuce Wraps	64
9. Chicken Fajita Bowl	65
10. Greek Style Chicken Kebabs	65
11. Thai Coconut Shrimp Curry	66
12. Grilled Chicken with Roasted Vegetables	66
13. Salmon with Lemon Herb Sauce	67
14. Beef stir-fry with Broccoli	67
15. Vegan Sweet Potato and Black Bean Chili	68
16. Lemon and Garlic Shrimp and Asparagus	68
17. Turkey Meatloaf with Green Beans	69
18. Vegan Tofu Stir-Fry	69
19. Baked Cod with Spinach	70
20. Chicken and Quinoa Stir-Fry	70
21. Vegan Coconut Curry with Chickpeas	71
22. Teriyaki Sauce-Glazed Salmon with Green Beans	71
23. Lemon and Garlic Grilled Chicken with Asparagus	72
24. Herb-Crusted Cod with Steamed Broccoli	72
25. Grilled Steak with Chimichurri Sauce	73
CHAPTER 7: 4-WEEK MEAL PLAN AND	74
GROCERY LIST	76
CONCLUSION	83
REFERENCES	84
RECIPE INDEX	86

INTRODUCTION

Have you ever wondered how a simple shift in your eating habits can transform your body and mind? A high-protein diet isn't just a trend; it's a powerful approach to achieving weight loss, muscle growth, and overall well-being. By focusing on a higher proportion of calories from protein while limiting fats and carbohydrates, this nutritional strategy offers flexibility and results. You can incorporate both high-fat protein and lean protein in your diet. Vegans mostly consume lean protein sources in the form of lentils, beans, tofu, seeds etc. However, meat lovers can cherish various options of meat like chicken, turkey, lamb, seafood, beef, etc.

Restricting carbs from the diet can be difficult, but science is here to the rescue. Science has progressed a lot over time and it has made everything logical for humans. Any goal or necessity can be fulfilled by bringing innovation on the page. Innovation and newly fangled ideas can do wonders. For instance, having specific health goals can be achieved today because science has provided all the legitimate methods to unlock your goal. You have got all the instruments like measuring tools, authentic information and technology in your hand in the form of health applications like myfitnesspal. All these things can make your accessible and easily achievable.
Planning is essential when making the switch from one diet to a high-protein one to make sure the change is long-lasting and successful. Treat your body gently!

If you make changes to it abruptly then it might respond negatively so it is advised to bring the change gradually. High-fat protein foods take a lot of time to digest and these also have high thermal effect. So, don't overburden your body by increasing the amount all of a sudden. Your meals in a day ideally should include both lean and fat-protein sources. Besides this, aim for fibre-rich carbs instead of refined carbs to keep your energy levels stable while you eat more protein.

At its core, a high-protein, low-carb diet is not just about restriction; it's about creating a balance that works for you. By gradually incorporating protein-rich foods and replacing refined carbs with nutrient-dense options, you can build a sustainable and enjoyable eating routine. This book is here to guide you every step of the way, starting with an understanding of the diet's fundamentals, followed by practical meal plans, grocery lists, and a collection of delicious recipes to help you achieve your goals. Let's begin this journey together toward a healthier, stronger, and more energized you!

CHAPTER 1:
GETTING STARTED WITH LOW-CARB, HIGH-PROTEIN LIVING

Our diet is composed of macronutrients and micronutrients (vitamins and minerals). Three macronutrients are carbohydrates, fats, and protein. The average recommended percentages for an individual are 45-65% for carbohydrates, 20-35% for fats and 10-35% for protein. These percentages are termed Acceptable Macronutrient Distribution Ranges (AMDR) in the nutrition science terminology. AMDRs can be tailored according to the specific health goal or health condition of a person (1).

For example, in the keto diet, zero carbs are given along with high protein and high-fat content. Besides this for a health condition like cardiovascular disease low-fat diet is advised for the person. Now, you have the concept that these percentages are adjusted according to the preferences and needs of a person. Moreover, the type of the macronutrient also varies.

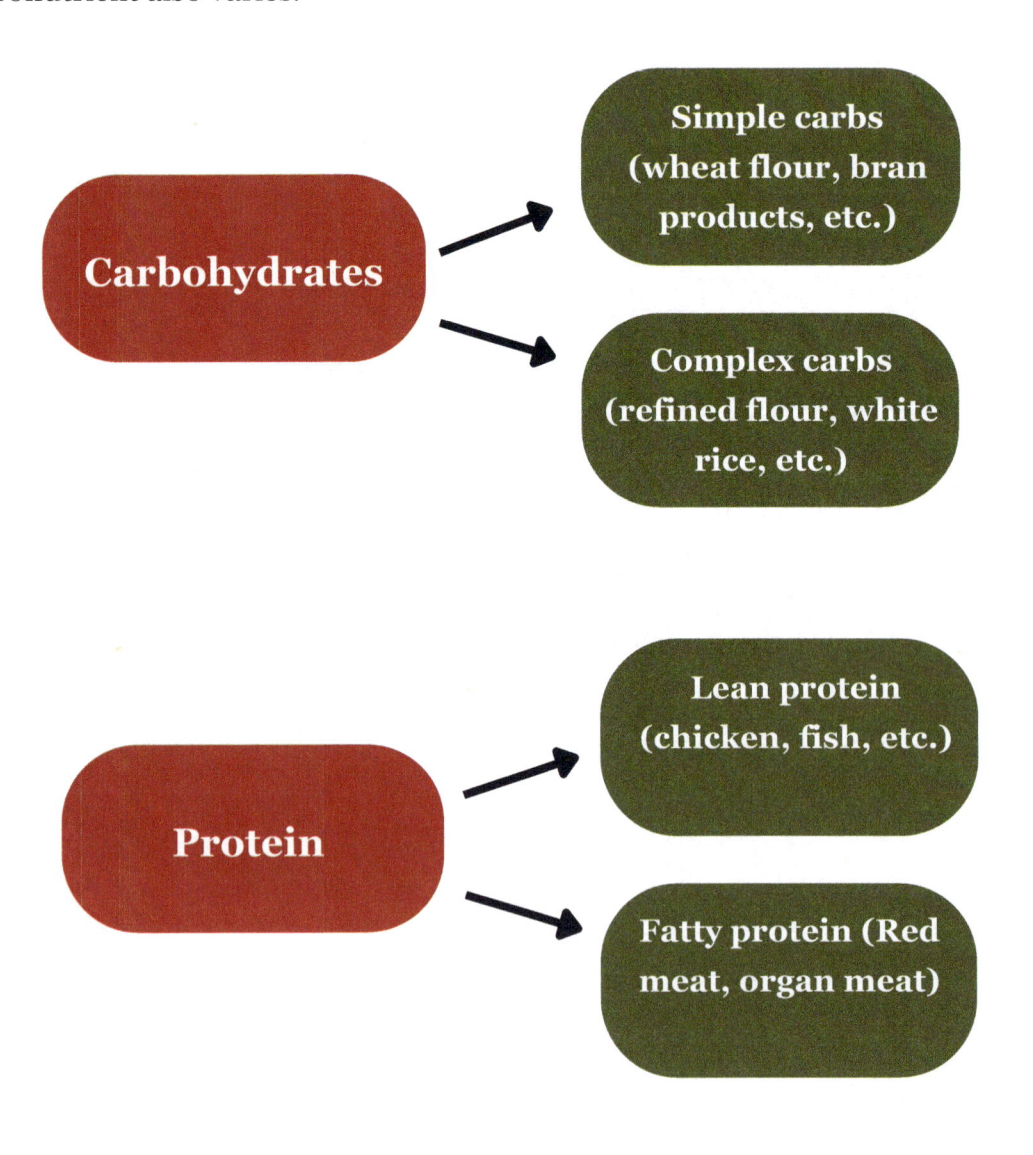

Carbohydrates
- Simple carbs (wheat flour, bran products, etc.)
- Complex carbs (refined flour, white rice, etc.)

Protein
- Lean protein (chicken, fish, etc.)
- Fatty protein (Red meat, organ meat)

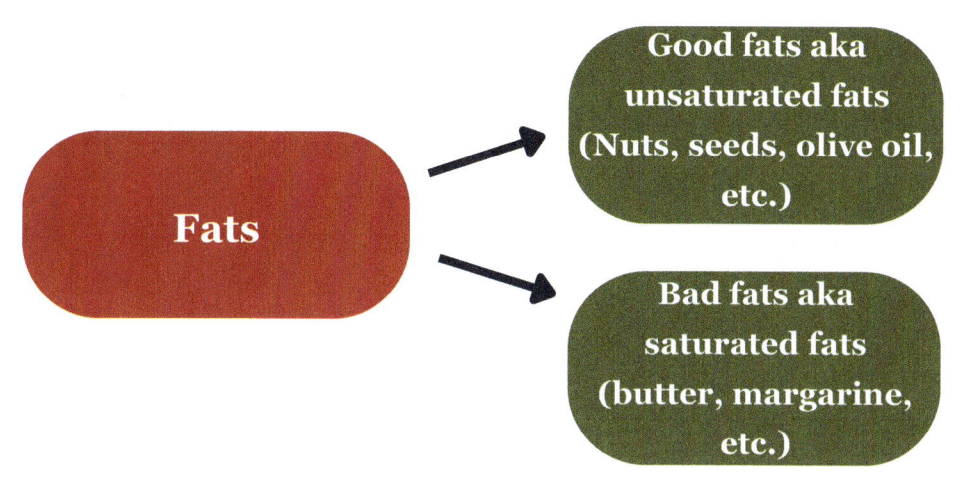

```
   ┌──────┐         ┌─────────────────────┐
   │      │────────▶│ Good fats aka       │
   │ Fats │         │ unsaturated fats    │
   │      │         │ (Nuts, seeds, olive oil, etc.) │
   │      │────────▶│ Bad fats aka        │
   └──────┘         │ saturated fats      │
                    │ (butter, margarine, etc.) │
                    └─────────────────────┘
```

Furthermore, many cultural and regional dietary patterns have unique AMDRs. For example, the mediterranean diet is specifically rich in whole grains, nuts, olive oil, seafood, fruits and vegetables. In contrast, the Western diet is high in processed foods, red meat and refined carbohydrates.

Just like that, people nowadays tend to opt for low-carb and high-protein diets. This book will thoroughly explain which people opt for this proportion of carbs and protein and what are its health outcomes.

Why Low-Carb, High-Protein?

In a low-carb diet, the carbohydrates are restricted to 26% of the daily intake of a standard 2000-calorie diet. It means that you are allowed to consume 130g of carbohydrates in a day.

The normal protein intake can be planned according to the 0.8g/kg weight of an individual. However, in the high protein diet, this amount is increased. Also, remember that when the amount of carbohydrates is reduced then a bit proportion of fats is increased to compensate for the energy requirements.

There are some of the diets that are based on these proportions:

Keto diet:

This diet comprises only 5% carbohydrates and a high content of protein and fats. The Keto diet was first originated to treat epilepsy patients. However, in current times it has got the limelight because of its fantastic results for weight loss.

According to him, you should use your hand and eye to portion your meal plate. This diet doesn't require strict grammage of the macronutrients.

He suggested to divide the plate into three parts.

• **Part 1:** 1/3 of the part should be of lean protein. Lean protein doesn't increase triglycerides or cholesterol levels and is safe for heart health.

• **Part 2:** 2/3 of the plate should be of carbohydrates. Here, you need to make sure that you are eating low glycemic index carbohydrates. These food sources do not spike up your blood sugar levels once they get absorbed in the blood.

Besides this, add a dash of fats to the plate. Monosaturated fats like avocado, olive oil, nuts and seeds are recommended for this. These are so beneficial for the heart health. Another method to design the plate is the zone block method:

According to this, males are allowed to eat 14 zones in a day and females are allowed to eat 11 zones per day.

How Does a Single Block Appear?

- Protein block: 7 grams of protein
- Carbs block: 9 grams of carbohydrates
- Fats block: 1.5 grams of fat (if you eat animal protein) or 3 grams of fat (if you eat vegetarian protein)

This method is a bit tricky because you need to check out the food content of everything that you eat.

Recommended protein sources:

- Turkey breast and skinless chicken
- Shellfish and fish
- Tofu, soy products, and vegetarian protein
- Egg whites
- Cheeses with less fat
- Low-fat yoghurt and milk

Recommended carbohydrate sources:
- Berries, oranges, plums, apples, and other fruits;
- Vegetables include cucumbers, peppers, spinach, tomatoes, mushrooms, yellow squash, and chickpeas.
- In grains, barley and oats are encouraged to eat.

Recommended fat sources:
- Avocados
- Nuts including pistachios, almonds, cashews, peanuts, and macadamia
- Peanut butter
- Tahini
- Oils like olive oil, peanut oil, sesame oil, and canola oil

Foods that are strictly prohibited in this diet are given in the table:

Food groups	Sources
Starchy vegetables	Potato, corn, carrots, peas
Refined and processed carbs	Pasta, noodles, bagels, bread and white flour products.
Soft drinks	Both sweetened and sugar-free drinks are not allowed.
Coffee and tea	Allowed only in moderation.
Processed foods	Muffins, cakes, etc.
High-sugar foods (Glycemic index)	Bananas, raisins, dried fruit, mango, raisin, and grapes.

Another familiar diet is the Sugar Busters diet;

Sugar Busters Diet:

It is a low-carb diet that focuses on cutting back on sugar and refined carbs to balance blood sugar levels, aid in weight loss, and enhance health (3). The diet's premise is that eating too many sugary and high-glycemic meals causes weight gain and other health problems.

It is founded on the idea that sugar is "toxic" and promotes weight gain by raising insulin levels, a hormone responsible for transporting sugar from the blood into cells. Insulin also regulates energy storage in the body, and studies have shown that consistently elevated insulin levels are associated with weight gain.

Benefits of a Low-Carb, high-protein diet

This dietary approach has legit health benefits that can improve your quality of life:

Helps in weight loss

Weight loss is a real challenge for many people and is the talk of the town. Many people search for the secret recipe for losing weight. Well, it can be achieved by low carb and high-fat diet. Because it reduces hunger. The protein in the diet helps regulate hunger and calorie intake by promoting satiety. Moreover, a diet low in carbohydrates promotes the body's burning of fat for energy, which speeds up the process of fat loss (4).

Another perk is that during the weight loss process, you won't lose your muscle mass because the protein helps keep muscles intact.

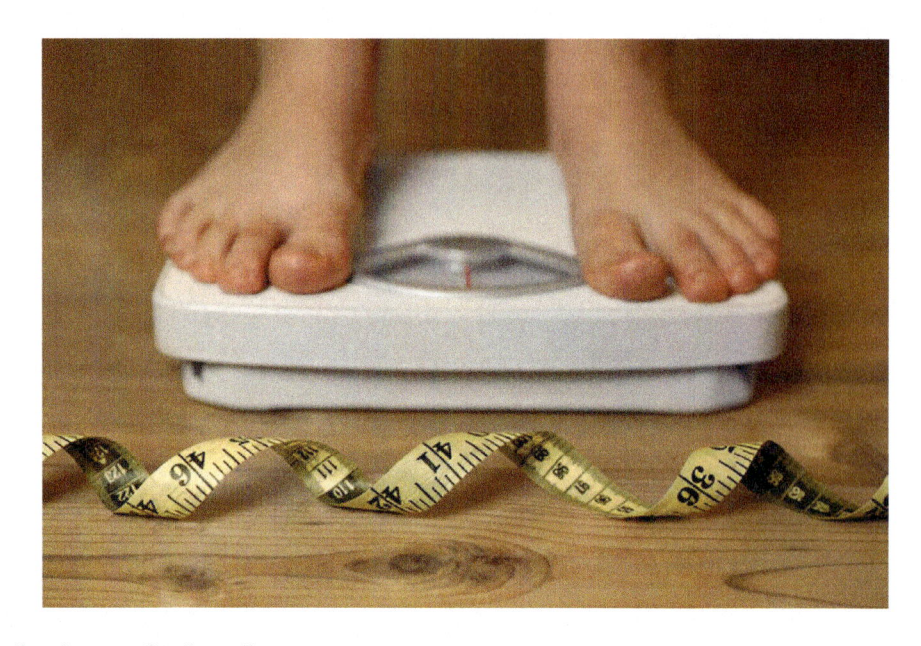

Better Regulation of Blood Sugar

It is a good dietary approach for diabetic patients and for those who are suffering from insulin resistance issues like Polycystic ovary syndrome patients.

Cutting carbs inhibits the increase in blood sugar and prevents a sharp spike in blood sugar. It also promotes greater insulin sensitivity. This property is highly advantageous for people with diabetes or prediabetes.

Encourages Physical Performance

Proteins are the building blocks of the muscles. Exercise and high protein intake are the secret key to growing your muscles. According to the National Academy of Medicine, an average human needs 0.8 g of protein per kg of their weight. But if you want to build more muscles then consume 1.6g/kg/day protein. The building and repairing of muscles need protein so it can help fitness enthusiasts. Besides this, protein and fat offer sustained energy for extended exercise.

For older adults

The muscle mass represents the weight occupied by our muscles in the body. After age 30, 3-5% of muscle mass drops gradually after a decade. That's why people above 50 look fragile and feeble. It is advised to them to focus more on protein intake to prevent muscle loss.

Note:

The muscle mass recommendation for men aged 40 to 49 years should be between 73% to 86%. Ranges for women are 62% to 73.5%.

Better Lipid Profile for Heart Health

Research indicates that low-carb diets raise HDL (good cholesterol) and lower triglycerides.

- **Decreased Inflammation:** Diets high in protein and low in carbohydrates can improve cardiovascular health by reducing inflammatory indicators.

Sustainability and Simplicity

- **Diminished Cravings:** Reducing carbohydrates frequently reduces cravings for processed meals and sugar.

 Flexible Eating: A concentration of foods high in protein offers a range of meal options, including plant-based proteins and lean meats.

Who should not follow this diet?

●Women who are pregnant or nursing should have a balanced diet rather than drastically cutting back on carbohydrates.

● **Individuals with kidney disease:** Diets high in protein should only be followed under a doctor's supervision because they can strain the kidneys.

●High-intensity athletes might need more carbohydrates to operate at their best.

● **People with eating disorders:** Strict dietary guidelines may make their illness worse.

Tips for Success

Shifting to a new dietary pattern can be challenging. Usually, at first, the individuals are motivated and have high spirits to continue the diet. But they lose because of reasons like cravings, unavailability of food or untimely meal planning. Therefore, this section has enlisted the practical tips that will make your transition journey smooth and good.

1.Make a Weekly Meal Plan

First of all, planning your meals is essential. Plan your meals for the week by using the cookbook's grocery lists and 4-week meal plan. This stops unhealthy decisions at the last minute.

Batch cooking

If you have a tough routine then you can do batch cooking to avoid the unnecessary hassle. Save time and ensure that you always have a nutritious dinner on hand, prepare recipes in large quantities.

Prepare Ingredients

To make everyday meal preparation easier, chop veggies, marinade proteins, and portion-out snacks.

2.Track Your Intake

Keep a food journal or use apps to record your meals and monitor your intake of fats, proteins, and carbohydrates.

3. Celebrate your Small Victories

Being hard on yourself can be frustrating!

So, enjoy the little achievements that you have got. For instance, if you have followed the meal plan accurately for a week then consider it as a progress and don't worry about how much weight you have lost. Beyond weight loss, other indicators of success include increased energy, improved attention span, and regular eating patterns.

4. Drink plenty of water

An important factor of a good diet also includes the hydration level of a person. But since it is not included in the meal it is often neglected. You can never ace any health goal without giving importance to hydration. Water is a basic necessity for the body. Maintaining proper hydration promotes general health and helps control appetite.
Here is a tip:

Include electrolytic homemade drinks to keep yourself hydrated and energized. Also include fruits and vegetables that are rich in water content for example watermelon and cucumber respectively.

5. Be creative and customize the meals

There is no hard and fast rule when you are following recipes given in this book. If you don't like the flavour of a particular ingredient then you can skip it. Moreover, if you are short on any food from the ingredient list then skip it or think of any suitable alternative.
Pay Attention to Your Body:
Everybody has various demands. Adapt the diet to your preferences and energy levels.

Try Different Recipes:
To keep meals interesting, try new recipes and modify existing ones. The cookbook gives a variety.
 Don't worry about being perfect; if you have a bad day, pick up where you left off.

6. Control Your Cravings

Make a treat plan:
To sate your sweet tooth healthily, try the low-carb dessert recipes in this book.
Remain Full:
Consuming adequate amounts of protein and healthy fats lowers the risk of giving in to cravings for carbohydrates.
Avoid trigger foods:
Determine which foods cause overindulgence and cut them out.

7. Incorporate exercise into routine

Physical activity is an integral ingredient that is required to have a healthy body. Being physical activity protects you from stress, ageing, muscle loss and metabolic diseases like diabetes, hypertension and cardiac issues.
Also, if you have set a goal to lose weight then pair your diet with cardio or strength exercise. Remember that sustained energy and muscular recovery are supported by a healthy diet and adequate hydration.

8. Keep Low-Carb Essentials in Your Pantry

- Keep basic ingredients on hand, such as olive oil, low-carb sweeteners, almond flour, and coconut flour.
- Stock up on high protein sources. Always keep lean meats, eggs, tofu, and shellfish on hand.
- Keep sugar-free snacks, nuts, and seeds on hand in case you get hungry in between meals.

Essential Ingredients and Tools

Protein sources

- Meat and poultry include chicken breast, turkey, lean beef, pork chops, and lamb.
- Seafood includes salmon, tuna, shrimp, cod, and scallops.
- Dairy products like cottage cheese, Greek yoghurt (unsweetened), and hard cheeses like parmesan and cheddar.
- Plant-based options include tofu, tempeh, seitan, and edamame.

Vegetables Low in Carbs

You should try to eat vegetables that have a low content of carbohydrates. But if you want to eat from the carb content then you should minimize the serving size of the food. Doing this will balance meeting your macronutrient goals.
Vegetables like bbell peppers, cucumbers, mushrooms, spinach, kale, broccoli, cauliflower, zucchini, and asparagus are excellent sources.

Food fat sources:

Fatty fish, avocado, almonds (moderately), seeds (sunflower, flax, and chia), and olive oil.

Flavor enhancers

- Spices and herbs: paprika, turmeric, ginger, garlic, basil, and rosemary.
- Mustard, spicy sauce, soy sauce, and vinegar are examples of low-carb condiments.
- Low-sodium broth or stock.

Low-carb sources for confectionary and desserts

- Coconut flour, almond flour, and ground flaxseeds for baking.
- Low-carb sweeteners like erythritol, monk fruit sweetener or stevia.
- Dark chocolate (85% cocoa).

Tools

Tools for Meal Prep

1. Food scale: For precise macros and portion management.
2. Containers for meal prep: Used to keep prepared meals and snacks.
3. Cups and spoons for measuring: To keep track of ingredients and serving sizes.

Cooking Utensils

1. A non-stick skillet or pan is ideal for cooking lean proteins without the addition of grease.
2. Large protein portions, soups, and stews can be easily prepared using an Instant Pot or Slow Cooker.
3. The best tool for cooking meat and veggies is a grill or grill pan.
4. A blender or food processor can be used to make low-carb meals, sauces, and protein drinks.
5. Vegetables can be cooked in a steamer basket without additional oil.
6. Air Fryer is excellent for producing low-carb, crispy dishes with less oil.

How to use this cookbook

Begin with the introduction

Learn about the benefits of a low-carb, high-protein diet and its guiding principles.

Go through the Success Tips

These are necessary to guarantee that the recipes and meal plans you receive match your dietary objectives.

Monitor Your progress

Maintain a Journal: Record your favourite recipes, any alterations, and your post-meal feelings.

Make Recipes Work for You

Portion Sizes: Modify recipes to meet your dietary requirements.
Substitutions: Use different products, including vegetarian or dairy-free choices, to accommodate dietary needs or personal preferences.

Explore the index

There are distinct sections within the cookbook:

☐ Breakfast: Easy and tasty way to start the day.
☐ Snacks: Low-carb, healthful options for lunchtime cravings or when on the run.
☐ Lunch Ideas: Well-rounded meals to sustain your energy levels.
☐ Soups and stews: Warm, nourishing, and high in protein.
☐ Dinner: Filling meals to help you healthily finish the day.

Check the essential tools

Tools are underrated in the cookbooks. However, these play a key role in preparing meals especially when you have to keep in mind the grammage of the food and the serving size. Make sure your kitchen is stocked and prepared for these dishes by consulting the section on essential ingredients and tools.

CHAPTER 2:
BREAKFAST RECIPES

1. Spinach and Egg Muffins

Prep Time: 5 min |Cook Time:20 min |Servings: 3 muffins

Ingredients:

- 3 large eggs
- ½ cup fresh spinach, chopped
- ½ cup feta cheese, crumbled
- ¼ cup heavy cream
- ¼ tsp salt
- ¼ tsp black pepper

Preparation:

1. Preheat the oven to 175°C and grease a muffin tin.
2. Whisk eggs and heavy cream.
3. Add spinach, feta, salt and pepper.
4. Pour the mixture evenly into muffin tin.
5. Bake for 20 minutes and serve.

Nutritional Facts:

Calories: 120| Carbs:2g | Fat:8g | Protein: 10g

2. Turkey and Avocado Breakfast Scramble

Prep Time: 5 min |Cook Time:10 min |Servings: 1

Ingredients:

- 2 large eggs
- ¼ cup ground turkey (cooked)
- ½ avocado, sliced
- ½ tbsp olive oil
- ¼ tsp garlic powder
- Salt and pepper, to taste

Preparation:

1. Sauté cooked ground turkey in olive oil for 2 minutes.
2. Whisk eggs with garlic powder, salt and pepper, then pour into skillet.
3. Stir until eggs are fully cooked.
4. Top with diced avocado and serve.

Nutritional Facts:

Calories: 300| Carbs:3g | Fat:20g | Protein: 25g

3. Cheesy Omelet with Spinach and Mushrooms

Prep Time: 5 min |Cook Time:10 min |Servings: 1

Ingredients:

- 3 large eggs
- ¼ cup shredded cheddar cheese
- ½ cup spinach, chopped
- ¼ cup mushrooms, sliced
- 1 tsp olive oil
- Salt and pepper, to taste

Preparation:

1. Cook mushrooms and spinach in heated oil for 2-3 minutes.
2. Whisk eggs with salt and pepper and pour over veggies.
3. Sprinkle cheese on top and cook until set.
4. Fold and serve immediately.

Nutritional Facts:

Calories: 280| Carbs:3g | Fat:22g | Protein: 20g

4. Salmon and Avocado Breakfast Bowl

Prep Time: 5 min |Cook Time: 5 min |Servings: 1

Ingredients:

- 3 oz smoked salmon
- ½ avocado, sliced
- 2 large boiled eggs, sliced
- 1 tbsp lemon juice
- 1 tsp olive oil
- Salt and pepper, to taste

Preparation:

1. Arrange salmon, boiled eggs and avocado in a bowl.
2. Drizzle with lemon juice and olive oil.
3. Season with salt and pepper and serve.

Nutritional Facts:

Calories: 350| Carbs:4g | Fat:26g | Protein: 25g

5. Greek Yogurt and Almond Butter Parfait

Prep Time: 5 min |Cook Time: None |Servings: 1

Ingredients:

- 1 cup plain Greek yogurt
- 1 tbsp almond butter
- 1 tsp chia seeds

Preparation:

1. Layer all the ingredients in a glass.
2. Refrigerate for one hour.
3. Serve chilled.

Nutritional Facts:

Calories: 200| Carbs: 5g | Fat: 10g | Protein: 18g

6. Sausage and Egg Breakfast Cups

Prep Time: 10 min |Cook Time: 20 min |Servings: 3 cups

Ingredients:

- 3 large eggs
- 3 sausage links (low-carb)
- ¼ cup shredded mozzarella cheese

Preparation:

1. Preheat the oven to 175°C and grease a muffin tin.
2. Cook sausage links and place one in each muffin cup.
3. Whisk eggs and pour over sausage.
4. Sprinkle with cheese and bake for 20 minutes.
5. Serve warm.

Nutritional Facts:

Calories: 150| Carbs: 1g | Fat: 11g | Protein: 12g

7. Almond Flour Waffles

Prep Time: 10 min |Cook Time: 20 min |Servings: 2

Ingredients:

- 2 large eggs
- ¼ cup almond flour
- ½ tsp baking powder
- 1 tbsp coconut oil
- ¼ cup unsweetened almond milk

Preparation:

1. Mix all ingredients until smooth.
2. Pour batter in waffle iron and cook until golden brown.

Nutritional Facts:

Calories: 200| Carbs: 4g | Fat: 16g | Protein: 10g

8. Bacon-Wrapped Asparagus

Prep Time: 5 min |Cook Time: 15 min |Servings: 4

Ingredients:

- 12 asparagus spears
- 6 slices bacon

Preparation:

1. Preheat oven to 200°C.
2. Wrap 2 asparagus spears with each slice of bacon.
3. Bake for 15 minutes until bacon is crispy.

Nutritional Facts:

Calories: 120| Carbs: 1g | Fat: 9g | Protein: 8g

9. Zucchini and Cheese Hash Browns

Prep Time: 10min |Cook Time: 10 min |Servings: 2

Ingredients:

- 1 medium zucchini, grated
- ¼ cup shredded cheese (cheddar or mozzarella)
- 1 egg
- ¼ tsp garlic powder

Preparation:

1. Squeeze excess moisture from zucchini.
2. Miz with cheese, egg and garlic powder.
3. Form patties and cook on a greased skillet for 3-4 minutes per side.

Nutritional Facts:

Calories: 150| Carbs: 3g | Fat: 10g | Protein: 10g

10. Chicken Breakfast Patties

Prep Time: 10min |Cook Time: 10 min |Servings: 4

Ingredients:

- 1 lb ground chicken
- 1 tsp dried parsley
- ½ tsp onion powder
- ¼ tsp garlic powder
- Salt and pepper to taste

Preparation:

1. Mix all ingredients in a bowl to form patties.
2. Cook in a greased skillet for 4-5 minutes each side.

Nutritional Facts:

Calories: 120| Carbs: 0g | Fat: 6g | Protein: 15g

11. Coconut Flour Pancakes

Prep Time: 10min | Cook Time: 10 min | Servings: 2

Ingredients:

- 2 large eggs
- 2 tbsp coconut flour
- ¼ cup unsweetened almond milk
- ¼ tsp baking powder

Preparation:

1. Mix all ingredients until smooth.
2. Cook small pancakes in a greased skillet, 2-3 minutes per side.

Nutritional Facts:

Calories: 170| Carbs: 0g | Fat: 6g | Protein: 15g

12. Mini Crustless Quiches

Prep Time: 10min | Cook Time: 25min | Servings: 3

Ingredients:

- 3 large eggs
- ¼ cup diced turkey
- ¼ cup chopped spinach
- ¼ cup shredded cheddar cheese

Preparation:

1. Preheat oven to 190°C. Grease a muffin tin.
2. In a bowl, whisk eggs and stir in turkey bacon, spinach and cheese.
3. Divide mixture evenly into muffin cups.
4. Bake for 25 minutes or until set.

Nutritional Facts:

Calories: 120| Carbs: 1g | Fat: 8g | Protein: 10g

13. Keto Breakfast Burrito Bowl

Prep Time: 5 min |Cook Time: 10 min |Servings: 2

Ingredients:

- 2 large eggs
- ½ cup cooked ground beef
- ¼ cup shredded cheese
- ½ avocado, diced
- 1 tsp olive oil

Preparation:

1. Heat olive oil in a skillet. Add ground beef and cook for 2-3 minutes.
2. Scramble eggs in same skillet.
3. Assemble beef, eggs, cheese and avocado in a bowl.

Nutritional Facts:

Calories: 350| Carbs:4g | Fat: 25g | Protein: 25g

14. Low-Carb Breakfast Pizza

Prep Time: 5 min |Cook Time: 15 min |Servings: 2

Ingredients:

- 2 low- carb tortillas
- 2 large eggs
- ¼ cup shredded mozzarella cheese
- ¼ cup diced bell peppers

Preparation:

1. Preheat oven to 190°C.
2. Crack an egg onto each tortilla, sprinkle with peppers and cheese.
3. Bake for 10-15 minutes and serve.

Nutritional Facts:

Calories: 180| Carbs:4g | Fat: 10g | Protein: 15g

15. Protein-Packed Veggie Omelet

Prep Time: 10 min |Cook Time: 15 min |Servings: 1

Ingredients:

- 3 large eggs
- 1 cup spinach, chopped
- ½ cup cherry tomatoes, halved
- ¼ cup feta cheese, crumbled
- 1 tsp olive oil
- Salt and pepper, to taste

Preparation:

1. Sauté spinach and cherry tomatoes in heated oil fir 2 minutes.
2. Whisk the eggs and pour them on vegetables and cook for 3-4 minutes until the bottom is set.
3. Sprinkle feta cheese on the top and fold the omelet.
4. Cook for an additional minute.
5. Serve warm.

Nutritional Facts:

Calories: 400| Carbs:12g | Fat: 25g | Protein: 32g

16. Chicken Breakfast Burrito

Prep Time: 10 min |Cook Time: 5 min |Servings: 1

Ingredients:

- 1 medium whole- grain tortilla (about 8 inches)
- ½ cup grilled chicken breast, shredded
- ¼ cup avocado, sliced
- ¼ cup black beans, cooked
- 3 tbsp shredded cheddar cheese
- 1 tbsp Greek yogurt
- 1 tsp olive oil

Preparation:

1. Warm the tortilla in a skillet over low heat.
2. Spread Greek yogurt on the tortilla.
3. Layer the rest of ingredients.
4. Roll the tortilla and toast for 2 minutes each side.
5. Serve warm.

Nutritional Facts:

Calories: 520| Carbs:40g | Fat: 18g | Protein: 45g

17. Peanut Butter Banana Oatmeal

Prep Time: 5 min |Cook Time: 5 min |Servings: 1

Ingredients:

- ½ cup rolled oats
- 1 cup almond milk (unsweetened)
- 1 medium banana, sliced
- 1 tbsp peanut butter
- 2 tsp chia seeds
- 2 tsp hemp seeds

Preparation:

1. Combine oats and almond milk in a saucepan and simmer for 5 minutes.
2. Transfer the cooked oats in a bowl.
3. Top with chia seeds, sliced banana, hemp seeds and peanut butter.

Nutritional Facts:

Calories: 480| Carbs:65g | Fat: 15g | Protein: 16g

18. Greek Yogurt Power Bowl

Prep Time: 5 min |Cook Time: None |Servings: 1

Ingredients:

- ¾ cup plain Greek yogurt
- ½ cup mixed berries (strawberries, blueberries, raspberries)
- 2 tbsp granola
- 1 tbsp almond butter
- 1 tsp chia seeds

Preparation:

1. Add Greek yogurt to a bowl.
2. Top with the remaining ingredients.
3. Serve immediately.

Nutritional Facts:

Calories: 340| Carbs:28g | Fat: 12g | Protein: 25g

19. Sweet Potato and Egg Breakfast Hash

Prep Time: 10 min |Cook Time: 15 minutes |Servings: 2

Ingredients:

- 1 medium sweet potato, diced
- ½ cup bell peppers, diced
- ½ cup zucchini, diced
- 1 tbsp olive oil
- 4 large eggs
- Salt and pepper to taste

Preparation:

1. Cook diced sweet potato and cook for 8-10 minutes.
2. Stir in bell peppers and zucchini and cook for another 5 minutes.
3. Create 4 small wells in the hash and crack egg into each well.
4. Cover and cook for 3-5 minutes.
5. Serve warm.

Nutritional Facts:

Calories: 330| Carbs:30g | Fat: 15g | Protein: 15g

20. Vegan Chocolate Protein Smoothie Bowl

Prep Time: 5 min |Cook Time: None |Servings: 1

Ingredients:

- 1 medium frozen banana
- 1 scoop vegan chocolate protein powder
- 1 tbsp unsweetened cocoa powder
- ½ cup almond milk
- 1 tbsp almond butter
- 1 tsp hemp seeds

Preparation:

1. Blend all the ingredients until smooth.
2. Pour into a bowl and top with toppings of your choice.
3. Serve immediately.

Nutritional Facts:

Calories: 380| Carbs:45g | Fat: 10g | Protein: 22g

21. High-Protein Pancakes

Prep Time: 5 min |Cook Time: 10 min |Servings: 1

Ingredients:

- ½ cup rolled oats
- ½ cup cottage cheese
- 2 large eggs
- 1 scoop vanilla protein powder
- 1 tsp baking powder
- ¼ tsp cinnamon

Preparation:

1. Blend all ingredients into a smooth batter.
2. Grease a non-stick skillet and heat over medium flame.
3. Pour small amounts of batter to form pancakes and cook for 2-3 minutes per side.
4. Serve with a drizzle of honey.

Nutritional Facts:

Calories: 320| Carbs:25g | Fat: 10g | Protein: 28g

22. Avocado Toast with Eggs

Prep Time: 5 min |Cook Time: 5 min |Servings: 1

Ingredients:

- 1 slice whole-grain bread
- ½ avocado, mashed
- 2 large eggs (poached/ fried or scrambled)
- Salt, pepper and chilli flakes to taste

Preparation:

1. Toast the bread until crispy.
2. Spread mashed avocado on the toast.
3. Top with eggs and season with salt, pepper and chilli flakes.

Nutritional Facts:

Calories: 350| Carbs:20g | Fat: 22g | Protein: 20g

23. Chia Pudding with Protein Boost

Prep Time: 5 min + Overnight Chill |Cook Time: None |Servings: 1

Ingredients:

- 3 tbsp chia seeds
- 1 cup almond milk
- ½ scoop vanilla protein powder
- ¼ cup fresh strawberries, sliced

Preparation:

1. In a jar, mix chia seeds, almond milk and protein powder.
2. Refrigerate overnight or for at least 4 hours.
3. Top with sliced strawberries before serving.

Nutritional Facts:

Calories: 300| Carbs:15g | Fat: 15g | Protein: 18g

24. Tofu Scramble with Vegetables

Prep Time: 5 min |Cook Time: 10 min |Servings: 1

Ingredients:

- 4 oz firm tofu, crumbled
- ½ cup bell pepper, diced
- ½ cup zucchini, diced
- 1 tsp olive oil
- ¼ tsp turmeric
- Salt and pepper, to taste

Preparation:

1. Sauté bell pepper and zucchini in heated oil for 3-4 minutes.
2. Add crumbled tofu, salt, turmeric and pepper.
3. Cook for another 5 minutes.
4. Serve warm.

Nutritional Facts:

Calories: 230| Carbs:10g | Fat: 12g | Protein: 18g

25. Spinach and Feta Omelet

Prep Time: 5 min |Cook Time: 5min |Servings: 1

Ingredients:

- 2 large eggs
- 1 tbsp milk
- ½ cup fresh spinach, chopped
- 2 tbsp crumbled feta cheese
- 1 tsp olive oil

Preparation:

1. Whisk eggs and milk in a bowl.
2. Heat olive oil in a non-stick skillet over medium heat,
3. Pour egg mixture into the skillet and cook until edges set.
4. Add spinach and feta cheese to one half of omelet.
5. Fold the other half and cook for 1-2 minutes.
6. Serve hot.

Nutritional Facts:

Calories: 200| Carbs:2g | Fat: 16g | Protein: 14g

CHAPTER 3:
SNACK RECIPES

1. Greek Yogurt Parfait with Berries and Nuts

Prep Time: 5 min |Cook Time: None |Servings: 1

Ingredients:

- 1 cup plain Greek yogurt (2%)
- ½ cup mixed berries (blueberries, raspberries)
- 2 tbsp chopped almonds or walnuts
- 1 tsp honey (optional)

Preparation:

1. Layer Greek yogurt, berries and nuts in a serving glass.
2. Drizzle honey on top.
3. Serve immediately.

Nutritional Facts:

Calories: 250| Carbs:20g | Fat: 9g | Protein: 18g

2. Hard-Boiled Eggs with Avocado Slices

Prep Time: 10min |Cook Time: None |Servings: 1

Ingredients:

- 2 hard- boiled eggs
- ½ medium avocado, sliced
- Pinch of salt and pepper

Preparation:

1. Slice the hard-boiled eggs in half.
2. Arrange with avocado slices on a plate.
3. Season with salt and pepper and serve.

Nutritional Facts:

Calories: 220| Carbs:6g | Fat: 16g | Protein: 14g

3. Protein-Packed Smoothie

Prep Time: 5min |Cook Time: None |Servings: 1

Ingredients:

- 1 cup unsweetened almond milk
- 1 scoop vanilla protein powder
- ½ medium banana
- 1 tbsp peanut butter
- 3-4 ice cubes

Preparation:

1. Blend all ingredients until smooth.
2. Pour into a glass and enjoy.

Nutritional Facts:

Calories: 280| Carbs:20g | Fat: 10g | Protein: 25g

4. Veggie sticks with Hummus

Prep Time: 5min |Cook Time: None |Servings: 1

Ingredients:

- 1 cup mixed veggie sticks (carrots, celery, cucumbers)
- 3 tbsp hummus

Preparation:

1. Arrange veggies sticks on a plate.
2. Serve with hummus as a dip.

Nutritional Facts:

Calories: 150| Carbs:12g | Fat: 10g | Protein: 4g

5. Cottage Cheese and Pineapple Bowl

Prep Time: 5min |Cook Time: None |Servings: 1

Ingredients:

- ½ cup low-fat cottage cheese
- ½ cup diced fresh pineapple
- 1 tbsp chia seeds

Preparation:

1. Combine all the ingredients in a bowl.
2. Serve chilled.

Nutritional Facts:

Calories: 190| Carbs:15g | Fat: 7g | Protein: 14g

6. Rice Cakes with Almond Butter and Banana

Prep Time: 5min |Cook Time: None |Servings: 1

Ingredients:

- 2 rice cakes
- 1 tbsp almond butter
- ½ banana, sliced

Preparation:

1. Spread almond butter on rice cakes.
2. Top with sliced banana and serve.

Nutritional Facts:

Calories: 210| Carbs:32g | Fat: 8g | Protein: 6g

7. Tuna Salad with Crackers

Prep Time: 5min |Cook Time: None |Servings: 1

Ingredients:

- 1 can tuna in water, drained (3 oz)
- 1 tbsp light mayonnaise
- 1 tsp mustard
- 5 whole-grain crackers

Preparation:

1. Mix tuna, mayonnaise and mustard in a bowl.
2. Serve with crackers.

Nutritional Facts:

Calories: 220| Carbs:12g | Fat: 8g | Protein: 25g

8. Apple Slices with Peanut Butter

Prep Time: 5min |Cook Time: None |Servings: 1

Ingredients:

- 1 medium apple, sliced
- 1 tbsp peanut butter

Preparation:

1. Spread peanut butter on apple slices.
2. Serve immediately.

Nutritional Facts:

Calories: 180| Carbs:25g | Fat: 7g | Protein: 3g

9. Vegan Energy Balls

Prep Time: 5min |Cook Time: None |Servings: 6 balls

Ingredients:

- 1 cup rolled oats
- 2 tbsp almond butter
- 2 tbsp maple syrup
- 1 tbsp chia seeds
- 1 tbsp cocoa powder

Preparation:

1. Mix all ingredients in a bowl until well combined.
2. Roll into balls and refrigerate for 30 minutes.
3. Store in an airtight container.

Nutritional Facts:

Calories: 90| Carbs:10g | Fat:4g | Protein: 3g

10. Trail Mix

Prep Time: 3 min |Cook Time: None |Servings: 1

Ingredients:

- 2 tbsp almonds
- 2 tbsp walnuts
- 1 tbsp dried cranberries
- 1 tbsp dark chocolate chips

Preparation:

1. Mix all ingredients in a bowl.
2. Enjoy as a portable snack.

Nutritional Facts:

Calories: 220| Carbs:14g | Fat: 17g | Protein: 5g

11. Cucumber and Hummus Bites

Prep Time: 3 min |Cook Time: None |Servings: 1

Ingredients:

- 1 small cucumber, sliced
- 2 tbsp hummus
- 1 tsp sesame seeds

Preparation:

1. Arrange cucumber slices on a plate.
2. Top each slice with a dollop of hummus.
3. Sprinkle sesame seeds on top for extra flavor.

Nutritional Facts:

Calories: 120| Carbs:12g | Fat:7g | Protein: 3g

12. Roasted Chickpeas

Prep Time: 5 min |Cook Time:30 min |Servings: 2

Ingredients:

- 1 cup canned chickpeas, rinsed and drained
- 1 tsp olive oil
- ½ tsp paprika
- ½ tsp garlic powder
- Pinch of salt

Preparation:

1. Preheat oven to 200°C.
2. Toss chickpeas with olive oil, garlic powder, paprika and salt.
3. Spread on a baking sheet and roast for 30 minutes.
4. Cool slightly and enjoy as a crunchy snack.

Nutritional Facts:

Calories: 120| Carbs:18g | Fat: 3g | Protein: 5g

13. Zucchini Chips with Parmesan

Prep Time: 10 min |Cook Time: 20 min |Servings: 2

Ingredients:

- 1 zucchini, thinly sliced
- ¼ cup grated Parmesan cheese
- 1 tsp olive oil

Preparation:

1. Preheat oven to 190°C.
2. Toss zucchini slices with olive oil and parmesan.
3. Bake on parchment- lined sheet for 20 minutes.

Nutritional Facts:

Calories: 100| Carbs: 3g | Fat: 6g | Protein: 7g

14. Turkey and Guacamole Bites

Prep Time: 10 min |Cook Time: None |Servings: 2

Ingredients:

- 4 slice deli turkey
- ¼ cup guacamole

Preparation:

1. Spread guacamole on turkey slices.
2. Roll up and serve.

Nutritional Facts:

Calories: 140| Carbs: 2g | Fat: 9g | Protein: 14g

15. Baked Parmesan Crisps

Prep Time: 5 min | Cook Time: 8 min | Servings: 4

Ingredients:

- 1 cup grated parmesan cheese

Preparation:

1. Place small piles of Parmesan on a parchment-lined baking sheet.
2. Bake for 8 minutes until golden and crispy.

Nutritional Facts:

Calories: 110 | Carbs: 0g | Fat: 8g | Protein: 9g

CHAPTER 4:
LUNCH RECIPES

1. Chicken and Spinach Stuffed Bell Peppers

Prep Time: 10 min | Cook Time: 20 min | Servings: 2

Ingredients:

- 2 medium bell peppers, half and deseeded
- 1 cup cooked shredded chicken
- 1 cup fresh spinach, chopped
- ¼ cup shredded mozzarella cheese
- ¼ tsp. garlic powder

Preparation:

1. Preheat oven to 190°C.
2. Mix chicken, cheese, garlic powder and spinach.
3. Stuff mixture into bell pepper halves.
4. Bake for 20 minutes and serve.

Nutritional Facts:

Calories: 240| Carbs: 6g | Fat: 10g | Protein: 30g

2. Salmon and Avocado Lettuce Wrap

Prep Time: 10 min | Cook Time: None | Servings: 2

Ingredients:

- 4 large lettuce leaves
- 1 cup cooked flaked salmon
- ½ avocado, sliced
- 1 tbsp lemon juice

Preparation:

1. Lay lettuce leaves flat and fill with salmon and avocado.
2. Drizzle with lemon juice.
3. Roll up and serve.

Nutritional Facts:

Calories: 210| Carbs: 4g | Fat: 12g | Protein: 25g

3. Eggplant and Chicken Caprese Bake

Prep Time: 10 min |Cook Time: 25 min |Servings: 2

Ingredients:

- 1 medium eggplant, sliced
- 1 cup cooked shredded chicken
- ½ cup diced tomatoes
- ¼ cup shredded mozzarella cheese
- 1 tsp olive oil

Preparation:

1. Preheat oven to 200°C.
2. Layer eggplant, tomatoes and chicken in a baking dish.
3. Sprinkle with mozzarella and drizzle with olive oil.
4. Bake for 25 minutes.
5. Serve warm.

Nutritional Facts:

Calories: 230| Carbs: 6g | Fat: 6g | Protein: 10g

4. Tuna and Cucumber Boats

Prep Time: 10 min |Cook Time: None |Servings: 2

Ingredients:

- 1 large cucumber, halved and deseeded
- 1 can tuna (5 oz), drained
- 2 tbsp mayonnaise
- 1 tbsp chopped fresh dill

Preparation:

1. Mix tuna, mayonnaise and dill.
2. Stuff the mixture into cucumber halves.
3. Serve immediately.

Nutritional Facts:

Calories: 200| Carbs: 3g | Fat: 10g | Protein: 25g

5. Shrimp and Cauliflower Rice Bowl

Prep Time: 10 min | Cook Time: 10 min | Servings: 1

Ingredients:

- ½ cup cooked shrimp
- ½ cup cauliflower rice
- ½ tbsp olive oil
- ¼ tsp paprika

Preparation:

1. Sauté cauliflower rice in heated olive oil for 5 minutes.
2. Add shrimp and paprika, cook for 2 more minutes.
3. Serve warm.

Nutritional Facts:

Calories: 220| Carbs: 5g | Fat: 10g | Protein: 25g

6. Grilled Chicken and Asparagus

Prep Time: 10 min | Cook Time: 15 min | Servings: 2

Ingredients:

- 2 small chicken breasts (4 oz each)
- 6 spears asparagus
- 1 tsp olive oil
- ¼ tsp garlic powder

Preparation:

1. Preheat grill.
2. Brush chicken and asparagus with olive oil and season with garlic powder.
3. Grill chicken for 6-7 minutes and asparagus for 5 minutes.
4. Serve!

Nutritional Facts:

Calories: 250| Carbs: 3g | Fat: 10g | Protein: 35g

7. Seared Tofu with Broccoli

Prep Time: 10 min |Cook Time: 15 min |Servings: 2

Ingredients:

- 1 cup firm tofu, cubed
- 1 cup broccoli florets
- 1 tbsp soy sauce
- 1 tsp sesame oil

Preparation:

1. Heat sesame oil in a skillet over medium heat.
2. Sear tofu cubes for 3-4 minutes each side.
3. Add soy sauce and broccoli, cook for 5 minutes.

Nutritional Facts:

Calories: 200| Carbs: 6g | Fat: 10g | Protein: 20g

8. Garlic and Rosemary Roasted Chicken Thighs

Prep Time: 10min |Cook Time: 12min |Servings: 1

Ingredients:

- 2 bone-in, skin on chicken thighs
- ½ tbsp olive oil
- 1 garlic clove, minced
- ½ tsp fresh rosemary, chopped
- ½ tbsp lemon juice

Preparation:

1. Preheat the oven to 190°C.
2. Rub chicken thighs with olive oil and season with rosemary, garlic, salt and pepper.
3. Roast chicken for 25 minutes and drizzle with lemon before serving.

Nutritional Facts:

Calories: 320| Carbs:2g | Fat: 23g | Protein: 24g

9. Beef and Bell Pepper Skewers

Prep Time: 10min |Cook Time: 10min |Servings: 2

Ingredients:

- 8 oz lean beef sirloin, cubed
- 1 tbsp olive oil
- 1 tsp smoked paprika
- 1 red bell pepper, cut into chunks
- 1 yellow bell pepper, cooked into chunks

Preparation:

1. Toss beef cubes with olive oil, paprika, salt and pepper.
2. Thread bell peppers and beef onto skewers.
3. Grill for 8-10 minutes, turning occasionally.
4. Serve hot.

Nutritional Facts:

Calories: 280| Carbs:5g | Fat: 15g | Protein: 28g

10. Turmeric and Ginger Shrimp Stir-Fry

Prep Time: 10 min |Cook Time: 10 min |Servings: 1

Ingredients:

- 6 oz shrimp, peeled and deveined
- 1 tsp olive oil
- ½ tsp fresh ginger
- 1/4th tsp ground turmeric
- ½ tbsp lime juice
- 1 cup baby spinach

Preparation:

1. Add ginger and turmeric in heated olive oil and stir for 30 seconds.
2. Now, add shrimp and cook for 3 minutes each side.
3. Add spinach and lime juice. Keep cooking until spinach wilts.
4. Season with salt and pepper and serve.

Nutritional Facts:

Calories: 210| Carbs: 5g | Fat: 6g | Protein: 30g

11. Ginger Soy Salmon

Prep Time: 10min | Cook Time: 8 min | Servings: 1

Ingredients:

- 1 salmon fillet (6 oz)
- 1 tbsp soy sauce
- 1 tsp grated ginger
- 1 tsp honey
- 1 tsp sesame oil

Preparation:

1. Combine soy sauce, ginger, honey and sesame oil in a bowl. Brush this mixture over salmon.
2. Grill the salmon for 4 minutes.

Nutritional Facts:

Calories: 290| Carbs: 4g | Fat: 14g | Protein: 28g

12. Balsamic Vinegar-Glazed Chicken Drumsticks

Prep Time: 10min | Cook Time: 20min | Servings: 1

Ingredients:

- 3 chicken drumsticks
- ½ tbsp olive oil
- 1 tbsp balsamic vinegar
- ½ tsp honey
- ½ tsp Dijon mustard

Preparation:

1. In a bowl, mix vinegar, honey and Dijon mustard and set this glaze aside.
2. Toss chicken drumsticks with olive oil salt and pepper.
3. Bake for 20 minutes at 200°C.
4. Brush drumsticks with glaze and serve.

Nutritional Facts:

Calories: 300| Carbs:5g | Fat: 16g | Protein: 28g

13. Herb-Infused Lamb Meatballs

Prep Time: 10min | Cook Time: 15min | Servings: 1

Ingredients:

- 4 oz ground lamb
- ½ tsp dried oregano
- ½ tsp dried parsley
- 1 garlic clove, minced
- ½ tbsp olive oil

Preparation:

1. Combine ground lamb, parsley, oregano, garlic, salt and pepper.
2. Form into 4 meatballs.
3. Heat olive oil in a skillet and cook meatballs for 12-15 minutes or until fully cooked.
4. Serve.

Nutritional Facts:

Calories: 290| Carbs:1g | Fat: 21g | Protein: 22g

14. Grilled Chicken and Quinoa Bowl

Prep Time: 10 min | Cook Time: 15 min | Servings: 2

Ingredients:

- 1 cup cooked quinoa
- 2 medium chicken breasts, grilled and sliced
- 1 cup steamed broccoli florets
- ½ cup cherry tomatoes, halved
- 2 tbsp olive oil
- 1 tbsp lemon juice
- Salt and pepper, to taste

Preparation:

1. Prepare quinoa according to package instructions.
2. Grill the chicken breast until fully cooked and slice into strips.
3. In a bowl, combine quinoa, broccoli, chicken and cherry tomatoes.
4. Drizzle with olive oil and lemon juice.
5. Season with salt and pepper and serve.

Nutritional Facts:

Calories: 390| Carbs:30g | Fat: 12g | Protein: 35g

15. Vegan Lentil Salad

Prep Time: 10 min|Cook Time: None |Servings: 2

Ingredients:

- 1 cup cooked green lentils
- 1 cup spinach
- ½ cup cucumber, diced
- ¼ cup red onion, thinly sliced
- 1 tbsp olive oil
- 1 tbsp balsamic vinegar
- 1 tsp Dijon mustard
- Salt and pepper, to taste

Preparation:

1. In a large bowl, mixed cook lentils, arugula, cucumber and red onions.
2. In a small bowl, whisk together olive oil, balsamic vinegar, Dijon mustard, salt and pepper.
3. Pour this dressing over the salad.
4. Toss to combine.

Nutritional Facts:

Calories: 280| Carbs:35g | Fat: 8g | Protein: 16g

16. Turkey and Avocado Wrap

Prep Time: 10 min|Cook Time: None |Servings: 1

Ingredients:

- 1 whole-grain tortilla
- 3 oz sliced turkey breasts
- ¼ avocado, mashed
- ½ cup mixed greens
- 2 slices tomato
- 1 tsp Dijon mustard

Preparation:

1. Spread mashed avocado over the tortilla.
2. Layer mixed greens, turkey, tomato slices and mustard.
3. Roll the tortilla tightly, slice in half and serve.

Nutritional Facts:

Calories: 320| Carbs:25g | Fat: 10g | Protein: 28g

17. Shrimp Stir-Fry

Prep Time: 10 min | Cook Time: 10 min | Servings: 2

Ingredients:
- 12 oz shrimp, peeled and deveined
- 2 cups mixed vegetables (bell peppers, snap pears, carrots)
- 1 tbsp olive oil
- 2 tbsp soy sauce
- 1 tsp garlic, minced
- 2 tsp ginger, grated

Preparation:
1. Heat olive oil in a large skillet or wok over medium- high heat.
2. Add shrimp and cook until pink, about 3-4 minutes. Remove and set aside.
3. Add garlic, ginger and mixed vegetables to skillet and stir fry for 5-7 minutes.
4. Add shrimps to the skillet.
5. Stir in soy sauce and cook for 1-2 minutes.
6. Serve immediately.

Nutritional Facts:
Calories: 290| Carbs:12 g | Fat: 10g | Protein: 35g

18. Grilled Salmon Salad

Prep Time: 10 min | Cook Time: 10 min | Servings: 2

Ingredients:
- 2 salmon filets (4 oz each)
- 4 cups mixed salad greens
- ½ avocado, sliced
- ½ cup cherry tomatoes, halved
- 2 tbsp olive oil
- 1 tbsp lemon juice
- Salt and pepper, to taste

Preparation:
1. Grill salmon fillets over medium heat for 4-5 minutes each side.
2. Arrange salad greens, avocado, cherry tomatoes on plates.
3. Place the grill salmon on top.
4. Drizzle with olive oil and lemon juice.
5. Season with salt and pepper and serve.

Nutritional Facts:
Calories: 400| Carbs:10g | Fat: 25g | Protein: 35g

19. Vegan Chickpea Curry

Prep Time: 10 min |Cook Time: 20 min |Servings: 2

Ingredients:

- 1 cup canned chickpeas, drained and rinsed
- 1 cup canned diced tomatoes
- 1 cup coconut milk
- 1 cup spinach
- 1 tsp curry powder
- 1 tsp olive oil
- Salt and pepper to taste

Preparation:

1. Heat olive oil in a pot. Add curry powder and toss for 30 seconds.
2. Stir in tomatoes, coconut and chickpeas. Simmer for 15 minutes.
3. Add spinach and cook until wilted.
4. Add salt and pepper to taste and serve warm.

Nutritional Facts:

Calories: 320| Carbs:30g | Fat: 18g | Protein: 12g

20. Chicken and Sweet Potato Bowl

Prep Time: 10 min |Cook Time: 20 min |Servings: 2

Ingredients:

- 1 medium chicken breast, grilled and diced
- 2 medium sweet potatoes, diced and roasted
- 1 cup steamed broccoli
- ¼ cup cherry tomatoes
- 2 tbsp olive oil
- 1 tsp paprika
- Salt and pepper, to taste

Preparation:

1. Roast sweet potatoes at 200°C for 20 minutes, drizzled with 1 tbsp olive oil, paprika, salt and pepper.
2. Grill the chicken breast and dice.
3. Combine everything in a bowl.
4. Drizzle with remaining oil and serve.

Nutritional Facts:

Calories: 380| Carbs:28g | Fat: 12g | Protein: 35g

21. Vegan Buddha Bowl

Prep Time: 10 min |Cook Time: 10 min |Servings: 2

Ingredients:

- 1 cup cooked quinoa
- ½ cup roasted chickpeas
- 1 cup steamed kale
- ½ avocado, sliced
- 2 tbsp tahini
- 1 tbsp lemon juice

Preparation:

1. Assemble bowls with chickpeas, quinoa, avocado and kale.
2. Mix tahini and lemon juice to make a dressing,
3. Drizzle dressing over the bowl and serve.

Nutritional Facts:

Calories: 350| Carbs:35g | Fat: 15g | Protein: 15g

22. Turkey Meatballs and Zoodles

Prep Time: 10 min |Cook Time: 15min |Servings: 2

Ingredients:

- 8 oz ground turkey
- 2 medium zucchinis, spiralized
- ½ cup marinara sauce
- 1 tsp garlic powder
- 1 tbsp olive oil

Preparation:

1. Form turkey into small meatballs, seasoning with garlic powder.
2. Cook meatballs in a skillet with olive oil until browned.
3. Add marinara sauce and simmer for 10 minutes.
4. Serve meatballs over zucchini noodles.

Nutritional Facts:

Calories: 290| Carbs:10g | Fat: 15g | Protein: 28g

23. Quinoa Stuffed Bell Peppers

Prep Time: 15 min | Cook Time: 25min | Servings: 2

Ingredients:

- 2 large bell peppers, halved and deseeded
- 1 cup cooked quinoa
- ½ cup black beans
- ½ cup diced tomatoes
- 1 tsp cumin
- 1 tbsp olive oil

Preparation:

1. Preheat oven to 190°C.
2. Mix quinoa, tomato, black beans and cumin in a bowl to form a mixture.
3. Stuff bell peppers with the mixture.
4. Bake for 25 minutes and serve.

Nutritional Facts:

Calories: 280| Carbs:40g | Fat: 6g | Protein: 12g

24. Lentil and Kale Soup

Prep Time: 10 min | Cook Time: 25min | Servings: 1

Ingredients:

- ½ cup cooked lentils
- 1 cup kale, chopped
- 1 cup vegetable broth
- 1 garlic clove, minced
- ½ tsp paprika
- 1 tsp olive oil

Preparation:

1. Heat olive oil in pot and sauté garlic for 2 minutes.
2. Add cooked lentils, vegetable broth and paprika.
3. Simmer for 10 minutes.
4. Add kale and cook for another 5 minutes.
5. Serve hot.

Nutritional Facts:

Calories: 200| Carbs:28g | Fat: 4g | Protein: 12g

25. Chicken and Chickpea Salad

Prep Time: 10 min | Cook Time: None | Servings: 1

Ingredients:

- 3 oz grilled chicken breast, sliced
- ½ cup canned chickpeas, drained and rinsed
- 1 cup arugula
- 1 tbsp olive oil
- 1 tbsp lemon juice
- Salt and pepper, to taste

Preparation:

1. Combine chicken, chickpeas and arugula in a bowl.
2. Drizzle with olive oil and lemon juice.
3. Toss gently and serve.

Nutritional Facts:

Calories: 320| Carbs:18g | Fat: 14g | Protein: 28g

CHAPTER 5:
SOUP AND STEWS

1. Chicken Zoodle Soup

Prep Time: 10 min |Cook Time: 15min |Servings: 2

Ingredients:

- 2 cups chicken broth
- 1 cup cooked shredded chicken
- 1 medium zucchini, spiralized
- ¼ tsp garlic powder
- ¼ tsp dried thyme

Preparation:

1. Heat chicken broth in a pot over medium heat.
2. Add shredded chicken, garlic powder and thyme.
3. Simmer for 10 minutes and add zucchini noodles.
4. Cook for additional 2-3 minutes and serve.

Nutritional Facts:

Calories: 120| Carbs:3g | Fat: 3g | Protein: 20g

2. Beef and Mushroom Stew

Prep Time: 10 min |Cook Time: 25min |Servings: 2

Ingredients:

- 8 oz beef stew meat
- 1 cup sliced mushrooms
- 1 cup beef broth
- ¼ cup chopped onion
- 1 tbsp olive oil

Preparation:

1. Heat olive oil in a pot and brown beef on all sides.
2. Add mushrooms, onion and beef broth.
3. Simmer for 20 minutes.
4. Serve warm.

Nutritional Facts:

Calories: 280| Carbs:5g | Fat: 14g | Protein: 30g

3. Spicy Shrimp Coconut Soup

Prep Time: 10 min |Cook Time: 10min |Servings: 2

Ingredients:

- 1 cup shrimp, peeled and deveined
- 1 cup unsweetened coconut milk
- 1 cup chicken broth
- ¼ tsp red flakes
- ½ tsp lime juice

Preparation:

1. Heat coconut milk and broth in a saucepan over medium heat.
2. Add shrimp and flakes and cook for additional 5 minutes.
3. Stir in lime juice and serve hot.

Nutritional Facts:

Calories: 220| Carbs:3g | Fat: 12g | Protein: 25g

4. Turkey and Spinach Soup

Prep Time: 10 min |Cook Time: 15min |Servings: 2

Ingredients:

- 8 oz ground turkey
- 2 cups chicken broth
- 1 cup fresh spinach
- ¼ tsp garlic powder

Preparation:

1. Cook turkey in a pot until browned.
2. Add chicken broth and garlic powder.
3. Simmer for 10 minutes.
4. Stir in spinach and cook for 2 minutes.

Nutritional Facts:

Calories: 210| Carbs:2g | Fat: 9g | Protein: 30g

5. Creamy Cauliflower and Chicken Soup

Prep Time: 10 min |Cook Time: 20 min |Servings: 2

Ingredients:

- 1 cup cooked shredded chicken
- 2 cups cauliflower florets
- 2 cups chicken broth
- ¼ cup unsweetened almond milk

Preparation:

1. Cook cauliflower in chicken broth for 15 minutes.
2. Blend mixture until smooth.
3. Stir in almond milk and shredded chicken.

Nutritional Facts:

Calories: 180| Carbs:5g | Fat: 6g | Protein: 25g

6. Egg Drop Soup with Spinach

Prep Time: 5 min |Cook Time: 10min |Servings: 2

Ingredients:

- 2 cups chicken broth
- 2 eggs, beaten
- 1 cup fresh spinach
- ¼ tsp sesame oil

Preparation:

1. Heat chicken broth in a bot until it simmers.
2. Slowly add beaten eggs while stirring,
3. Stir in spinach and cook for 2 more minutes.
4. Serve hot.

Nutritional Facts:

Calories: 120| Carbs:2g | Fat: 7g | Protein: 12g

7. Beef Bone Broth Soup

Prep Time: 10 min |Cook Time: 15 min |Servings: 2

Ingredients:

- 2 cups beef bone broth
- ½ cup diced beef
- ½ cup diced celery
- ¼ cup diced onion

Preparation:

1. Heat broth in a pot.
2. Add the rest of ingredients and simmer for 15 minutes.

Nutritional Facts:

Calories: 200| Carbs:4g | Fat: 10g | Protein: 22g

8. Kale and Sausage Stew

Prep Time: 10 min |Cook Time: 20 min |Servings: 2

Ingredients:

- 2 chicken sausage, sliced
- 2 cups chopped kale
- 2 cups chicken broth
- ¼ tsp garlic powder

Preparation:

1. Brown sausage in a pot.
2. Add rest of ingredients and simmer for 15 minutes.

Nutritional Facts:

Calories: 230| Carbs:4g | Fat: 12g | Protein: 26g

9. Lemon and Dill Chicken Soup

Prep Time: 10 min |Cook Time: 15 min |Servings: 2

Ingredients:

- 1 cup shredded cooked chicken
- 2 cups chicken broth
- 1 tbsp fresh dill, chopped
- ½ tbsp lemon juice
- ½ cup diced celery

Preparation:

1. Heat chicken broth in a pot over medium heat.
2. Add the rest of ingredients.
3. Simmer for 15 minutes.
4. Serve warm.

Nutritional Facts:

Calories: 140| Carbs: 3g | Fat: 4g | Protein: 22g

10. Creamy Broccoli and Cheddar Soup

Prep Time: 10 min |Cook Time: 20 min |Servings: 2

Ingredients:

- 2 cups chopped broccoli
- 1 cup chicken broth
- ½ cup unsweetened almond milk
- ¼ cup shredded cheddar cheese

Preparation:

1. Cook broccoli in chicken broth for 15 minutes.
2. Blend the soup until smooth.
3. Stir in almond milk and cheddar cheese.
4. Simmer until cheese melts.

Nutritional Facts:

Calories: 180| Carbs: 6g | Fat: 10g | Protein: 15g

CHAPTER 6:
DINNER RECIPES

1. Mediterranean Baked Sardines

Prep Time: 10 min | Cook Time: 15 min | Servings: 1

Ingredients:

- 4 whole fresh sardines, cleaned
- ½ tbsp olive oil
- ½ tbsp fresh lemon juice
- ½ tsp dried oregano
- ¾ cup cherry tomatoes, halved

Preparation:

1. Preheat oven to 190°C.
2. Place sardines on baking sheet. Drizzle sardines with olive oil and lemon juice.
3. Scatter the cherry tomato halves around and sprinkle with oregano.
4. Bake for 12-15 mins and serve warm.

Nutritional Facts:

Calories: 210 | Carbs: 1g | Fat: 16g | Protein: 25g

2. Spicy Grilled Tuna Steak

Prep Time: 10min | Cook Time: 6 min | Servings: 1

Ingredients:

- 1 tuna steak
- ½ tbsp olive oil
- ½ tsp smoked paprika
- ½ tsp chili powder
- ½ tbsp lime juice
- Salt and pepper, to taste

Preparation:

1. Preheat the grill.
2. Drizzle olive oil over tuna steak and season with paprika, chili powder, salt and pepper.
3. Grill tuna steak for 3-4 minutes each side.
4. Drizzle with lime juice and serve.

Nutritional Facts:

Calories: 270 | Carbs: 4g | Fat: 15g | Protein: 30g

3. Teriyaki Sauce-Glazed Chicken Breast

Prep Time: 10min |Cook Time: 12min |Servings: 1

Ingredients:

- 1 boneless, chicken breast (6 oz)
- ½ tbsp coconut aminos
- ½ tsp honey
- 1 garlic clove, minced
- ½ tsp sesame oil

Preparation:

1. In a bowl, mix coconut aminos, sesame oil, honey and garlic to make teriyaki sauce.
2. Grill chicken breast for 5-6 minutes each side until fully tender.
3. Brush teriyaki sauce during last 2 minutes of cooking.
4. Slice and serve.

Nutritional Facts:

Calories: 240| Carbs:5g | Fat: 7g | Protein: 36g

4. Garlic Butter Shrimp and Zoodles

Prep Time: 10min |Cook Time: 12min |Servings: 1

Ingredients:

- 8 oz shrimp, peeled and deveined
- 2 medium zucchinis, spiralized
- 2 tbsp butter
- 2 cloves garlic, minced
- 1 tbsp lemon juice

Preparation:

1. Melt butter in a skillet over medium heat.
2. Add garlic and sauté for 1 minute.
3. Toss in shrimp and cook until pink, about 3 minutes per side.
4. Stir in lemon juice and zoodles, cooking for 2-3 minutes.

Nutritional Facts:

Calories: 280| Carbs:6g | Fat: 15g | Protein: 30g

5. Beef and Vegetable Stir-Fry

Prep Time: 10min |Cook Time: 15min |Servings: 1

Ingredients:

- 8 oz thinly sliced beef
- 1 cup broccoli florets
- ½ cup sliced bell peppers
- 1 tbsp soy sauce
- 1 tsp sesame oil

Preparation:

1. Heat sesame oil in a skillet, add beef and cook until browned.
2. Add broccoli, peppers and soy sauce stir fry for 5-7 minutes.

Nutritional Facts:

Calories: 300| Carbs:5g | Fat: 15g | Protein: 35g

6. Pesto chicken with Roasted Brussels Sprouts

Prep Time: 10min |Cook Time: 25min |Servings: 2

Ingredients:

- 2 chicken breasts
- 2 tbsp pesto (no sugar added)
- 1 cup brussels sprouts, halved
- 1 tsp olive oil

Preparation:

1. Preheat oven to 190°C.
2. Rub chicken with pesto and place on a baking sheet.
3. Toss Brussels with olive oil, add to the sheet and bake for 20-25 minutes.

Nutritional Facts:

Calories: 300| Carbs:5g | Fat: 15g | Protein: 35g

7. Cajun Salmon with Cabbage Slaw

Prep Time: 10min |Cook Time: 15min |Servings: 1

Ingredients:

- 2 salmon fillets (4 oz)
- 1 tsp Cajun seasoning
- 1 cup shredded cabbage
- 1 tbsp apple cider vinegar

Preparation:

1. Rub salmon with Cajun seasoning and bake at 190°C for 12-15 minutes.
2. Toss cabbage with apple cider vinegar and serve with salmon.

Nutritional Facts:

Calories: 280| Carbs:5g | Fat: 14g | Protein: 31g

8. Asian style Beef Lettuce Wraps

Prep Time: 10min |Cook Time: 10min |Servings: 1

Ingredients:

- 8 oz ground beef
- 1 tbsp soy sauce (low-sodium)
- 1 tsp sesame oil
- 6 large lettuce leaves

Preparation:

1. Brown beef in a skillet, add soy sauce and sesame oil.
2. Spoon beef mixture into lettuce leaves and serve as wraps.

Nutritional Facts:

Calories: 280| Carbs:5g | Fat: 15g | Protein: 30g

9. Chicken Fajita Bowl

Prep Time: 10min |Cook Time: 10min |Servings: 2

Ingredients:

- 6 oz chicken breast, sliced
- ½ bell pepper, sliced
- ½ cup cauliflower rice
- 1 tbsp fajita seasoning

Preparation:

1. Sauté bell pepper and chicken with fajita seasoning.
2. Serve with cauliflower rice.

Nutritional Facts:

Calories: 280| Carbs:5g | Fat: 15g | Protein: 30g

10. Greek Style Chicken Kebabs

Prep Time: 15min |Cook Time: 10min |Servings: 2

Ingredients:

- 6 oz chicken breast, cubed
- ½ tsp oregano
- ¼ cup Greek yogurt

Preparation:

1. Marinate chicken in yogurt and oregano for 10 minutes.
2. Thread onto skewers and grill for 3-4 minutes per side.

Nutritional Facts:

Calories: 260| Carbs:3g | Fat: 10g | Protein: 35g

11. Thai Coconut Shrimp Curry

Prep Time: 10min |Cook Time: 15min |Servings: 1

Ingredients:

- 6 shrimp, peeled and deveined
- ½ cup coconut milk
- 1 tbsp red curry paste

Preparation:

1. Sauté curry paste in a pan for 1 minute. Add shrimp and cook for 2-3 minutes,
2. Add coconut milk and simmer for 5 minutes.
3. Serve warm.

Nutritional Facts:

Calories: 250| Carbs:6g | Fat: 12g | Protein: 28g

12. Grilled Chicken with Roasted Vegetables

Prep Time: 10 min |Cook Time: 30 min |Servings: 2

Ingredients:

- 2 medium chicken breasts
- 2 cups mixed vegetables (zucchini, bell peppers and carrots)
- 2 tbsp olive oil
- 1 tsp garlic powder
- 1 tsp paprika
- Salt and pepper to taste

Preparation:

1. Preheat oven to 200°C.
2. Season chicken breasts with garlic powder, paprika, salt and pepper.
3. Toss mixed vegetables with olive oil, salt and pepper. Spread on a baking sheet.
4. Place chicken on the same baking sheet and roast for 25-30 minutes.
5. Serve warm.

Nutritional Facts:

Calories: 350| Carbs:15g | Fat: 14g | Protein: 38g

13. Salmon with Lemon Herb Sauce

Prep Time: 5 min | Cook Time: 10 min | Servings: 2

Ingredients:

- 2 salmon fillets (4 oz each)
- 1 tbsp olive oil
- 1 tbsp lemon juice
- 1 tsp fresh dill, chopped
- 1 cup steamed green beans

Preparation:

1. Heat olive oil in a skillet over medium heat.
2. Sear salmon fillets for 4-5 minutes each side.
3. Drizzle with lemon juice and sprinkle with dill.
4. Serve with green beans.

Nutritional Facts:

Calories: 320| Carbs:8g | Fat: 18g | Protein: 32g

14. Beef stir-fry with Broccoli

Prep Time: 10 min | Cook Time: 10 min | Servings: 2

Ingredients:

- 8 oz lean beef strips
- 2 cups broccoli florets
- 1 tbsp soy sauce
- 1 tbsp olive oil
- 1 tsp garlic, minced
- 1 tsp ginger, grated

Preparation:

1. Heat olive oil in a skillet over high heat.
2. Cook beef strips for 3-4 minutes. Remove and set aside.
3. Add broccoli, garlic and ginger to the skillet and cook for 5 minutes,
4. Return beef to skillet and add soy sauce.
5. Cook for additional 2 minutes.
6. Serve immediately.

Nutritional Facts:

Calories: 340| Carbs:10g | Fat: 18g | Protein: 34g

15. Vegan Sweet Potato and Black Bean Chili

Prep Time: 10 min |Cook Time: 20 min |Servings: 4

Ingredients:

- 1 medium sweet potato, diced
- 1 cup black beans
- 1 cup canned diced tomatoes
- 2 cups vegetable broth
- 1 tsp chili powder
- 1 tsp olive oil

Preparation:

1. Sauté sweet potatoes in heated oil for 5 minutes.
2. Add black beans, tomatoes, vegetable broth and chili powder.
3. Simmer for 15 minutes,
4. Serve hot.

Nutritional Facts:

Calories: 280| Carbs:50g | Fat: 4g | Protein: 10g

16. Lemon and Garlic Shrimp and Asparagus

Prep Time: 5 min |Cook Time: 10 min |Servings: 2

Ingredients:

- 12 oz shrimp, peeled and deveined
- 1 bunch asparagus, trimmed
- 1 tbsp olive oil
- 1 tsp garlic, minced
- 1 tsp ginger, grated

Preparation:

1. Heat olive oil in a skillet.
2. Cook shrimp with garlic for 4-5 minutes. Remove and set aside.
3. Add asparagus to skillet and cook for 5 minutes.
4. Return shrimp to skillet and lemon juice.
5. Cook for 1 more minute and serve.

Nutritional Facts:

Calories: 290| Carbs:50g | Fat: 10g | Protein: 35g

17. Turkey Meatloaf with Green Beans

Prep Time: 5 min |Cook Time: 40 min |Servings: 4

Ingredients:

- 1 lb. ground turkey
- ½ cup rolled oats
- 1 egg
- 1 tsp garlic powder
- 1 tsp onion powder
- 2 cup steamed green beans

Preparation:

1. Preheat oven to 190°C.
2. Mix ground turkey, oats, egg, garlic powder, onion powder in a bowl.
3. Form into a loaf and place on a baking sheet,
4. Bake for 40 minutes.
5. Serve with steamed green beans.

Nutritional Facts:

Calories: 280| Carbs:12g | Fat: 12g | Protein: 30g

18. Vegan Tofu Stir-Fry

Prep Time: 10 min |Cook Time: 10min |Servings: 2

Ingredients:

- 1 block firm tofu, cubed
- 2 cups mix vegetables (bell peppers, snap peas, carrots)
- 1 tbsp soy sauce
- 1 tsp sesame oi
- 1 tsp ginger, grated

Preparation:

1. Cook cubed tofu in heated oil for 5 minutes. Remove and set aside.
2. Add mixed vegetables and ginger to the skillet. Stir-fry for 5 minutes.
3. Return tofu to skillet and soy sauce.
4. Stir for 2 minutes.
5. Serve warm.

Nutritional Facts:

Calories: 300| Carbs:15g | Fat: 15g | Protein: 20g

19. Baked Cod with Spinach

Prep Time: 5 min |Cook Time: 15 min |Servings: 2

Ingredients:

- 2 cod fillets (4 oz each)
- 1 tbsp olive
- 1 cup spinach
- 1 tsp lemon zest
- Salt and pepper to taste

Preparation:

1. Preheat oven to 190°C.
2. Place cod fillets on a baking sheet.
3. Drizzle with olive oil, and sprinkle with lemon zest, salt and pepper.
4. Bake for 15 minutes.
5. Serve with sautéed spinach.

Nutritional Facts:

Calories: 250| Carbs:5g | Fat: 12g | Protein: 28g

20. Chicken and Quinoa Stir-Fry

Prep Time: 5 min |Cook Time: 15 min |Servings: 2

Ingredients:

- 2 medium chicken breasts, diced
- 1 cup cooked quinoa
- 1 cup mixed vegetables
- 1 tbsp soy sauce (low sodium)
- 1 tsp olive oil

Preparation:

1. Heat olive oil in a skillet over medium heat.
2. Cook chicken until golden. Remove and set aside.
3. Add vegetables to the skillet and stir- fry for 5 minutes.
4. Stir in quinoa, soy sauce and cooked chicken. Cook for 2 minutes.
5. Serve warm.

Nutritional Facts:

Calories: 320| Carbs:28g | Fat: 8g | Protein: 35g

21. Vegan Coconut Curry with Chickpeas

Prep Time: 10 min | Cook Time: 20 min | Servings: 2

Ingredients:

- 1 cup canned chickpeas, drained and rinsed
- 1 cup coconut milk
- 1 cup diced tomatoes
- 2 cups spinach
- 1 tsp curry powder

Preparation:

1. Heat curry powder in a pot for 30 seconds.
2. Add coconut milk, tomatoes and chickpeas. Simmer for 15 minutes.
3. Stir in spinach and cook until wilted.

Nutritional Facts:

Calories: 300 | Carbs: 30g | Fat: 14g | Protein: 12g

22. Teriyaki Sauce-Glazed Salmon with Green Beans

Prep Time: 5 min | Cook Time: 15 min | Servings: 1

Ingredients:

- 4 oz salmon fillet
- 1 tsp soy sauce
- 1 tsp honey/ maple syrup
- 1 tsp sesame oil
- 1 cup green beans, trimmed
- ½ tsp garlic minced

Preparation:

1. Preheat oven to 190°C.
2. Mix honey, soy sauce and sesame oil to make glaze.
3. Brush this glaze over salmon fillet.
4. Arrange salmon and green beans on a baking sheet and bake for 12-15 minutes.
5. Dish out and serve warm.
6.

Nutritional Facts:

Calories: 280 | Carbs: 6g | Fat: 15g | Protein: 30g

23. Lemon and Garlic Grilled Chicken with Asparagus

Prep Time: 5 min | Cook Time: 15 min | Servings: 1

Ingredients:

- 4 oz chicken breast
- 1 tsp olive oil
- ½ tsp garlic powder
- 1 tsp lemon juice
- 1 cup asparagus spears
- Salt and pepper, to taste

Preparation:

1. Rub chicken breast with lemon juice, olive oil, salt and pepper.
2. Grill chicken on medium heat until fully cooked.
3. Meanwhile, sauté asparagus in a skillet with touch of olive oil until tender.
4. Serve together.

Nutritional Facts:

Calories: 230| Carbs:3g | Fat: 10g | Protein: 30g

24. Herb-Crusted Cod with Steamed Broccoli

Prep Time: 5 min | Cook Time: 15 min | Servings: 1

Ingredients:

- 4 oz cod fillet
- 1 tsp olive oil
- ½ tsp dried thyme
- ½ tsp dried parsley
- 1 cup broccoli florets
- Salt and pepper to taste

Preparation:

1. Preheat oven to 190°C.
2. Rub cod fillet with olive oil, thyme and parsley.
3. Place fillet and broccoli on a baking sheet.
4. Bake for 15 minutes.

Nutritional Facts:

Calories: 320| Carbs:18g | Fat: 14g | Protein: 28g

25. Grilled Steak with Chimichurri Sauce

Prep Time: 10 min |Cook Time: 10 min |Servings: 2

Ingredients:

- 8 oz sirloin steak
- 1 tbsp olive oil
- 2 tbsp fresh parsley, chopped
- 1 clove garlic, minced

Preparation:

1. Grill steak for 4-5 minutes per side.
2. Mix parsley, garlic and olive oil for chimichurri and serve over steak.

Nutritional Facts:

Calories: 330| Carbs:2g | Fat: 18g | Protein: 35g

CHAPTER 7:
4-WEEK MEAL PLAN AND GROCERY LIST

WEEK 1

Day	Breakfast	Lunch	Dinner	Snack
1	Spinach and Egg Muffins	Chicken and Spinach Stuffed Bell Peppers	Mediterranean Baked Sardines	Greek Yogurt Parfait with Berries and Nuts
2	Turkey and Avocado Breakfast Scramble	Salmon and Avocado Lettuce wrap	Spicy Grilled Tuna Steak	Hard Boiled Eggs with Avocado Slices
3	Cheesy Omelet with Spinach and Mushrooms	Eggplant and Chicken Caprese Bake	Teriyaki Glazed Chicken Breast	Protein-Packed Smoothie
4	Salmon and Avocado Breakfast Bowl	Tuna and Cucumber Boats	Garlic Butter Shrimp and Zoodles	Veggie sticks with Hummus
5	Greek Yogurt and Almond Butter Parfait	Shrimp and Cauliflower Rice Bowl	Beef and Vegetable Stir-Fry	Cottage Cheese and Pineapple Bowl
6	Sausage and Egg Breakfast Cups	Grilled Chicken and Asparagus	Pesto chicken with Roasted Brussels Sprouts	Rice Cakes with Almond Butter and Banana
7	Almond Flour Waffles	Seared Tofu with Broccoli	Cajun Salmon with Cabbage Slaw	Tuna Salad with Crackers

GROCERY LIST

Fruits and Vegetables
Asparagus spears (6)
Avocado (2)
Banana (1)
Bell peppers (3)
Brussels sprouts (1 cup)
Cabbage (1 cup)
Carrots, celery, cucumbers (veggie sticks - 1 cup)
Cauliflower rice (½ cup)
Cherry tomatoes (¾ cup)
Cucumber (1)
Eggplant (1)
Garlic cloves (3)
Lettuce leaves (4)
Mixed berries (blueberries and raspberries - ½ cup)
Mushrooms (¼ cup)
Pineapple (½ cup)
Spinach (2 cups)
Tomatoes (½ cup)
Zucchini (2)

Proteins
Beef (8 oz)
Chicken breast (7)
Eggs (17)
Firm tofu (1 cup)
Sausage links (low-carb - 3)
Sardines (4)
Shrimp (10 oz)
Salmon fillets (4 fillets - 4 oz each)
Tuna (2 cans)
Tuna steak (1)
Turkey (grounded - ¼ cup)

Cereal and Starch
Almond flour (¼ cup)
Rice cakes (2)
Whole-grain crackers (5)

Dairy
Cheddar cheese (¼ cup)
Cottage cheese (low-fat - ½ cup)
Feta cheese (½ cup)
Heavy cream (¼ cup)
Plain Greek yogurt (2 cups)
Mozzarella cheese (¾ cup)

Non-Dairy
Almond milk (1¼ cups)
Nuts and Seeds
Almonds or walnuts (chopped - 2 tbsp)
Almond butter (2 tbsp)
Chia seeds (2 tbsp)
Peanut butter (1 tbsp)

Herbs, Condiments, Spices, and Oils
Apple cider vinegar (1 tbsp)
Black pepper (to taste)
Cajun seasoning (1 tsp)
Chili powder (½ tsp)
Coconut aminos (½ tbsp)
Dried oregano (½ tsp)
Fresh dill (1 tbsp)
Garlic powder (¾ tsp)
Honey (1½ tsp)
Lemon juice (3½ tbsp)
Lime juice (½ tbsp)
Mustard (1 tsp)
Olive oil (4 tbsp)
Paprika (¾ tsp)
Pesto (2 tbsp)
Salt (to taste)
Sesame oil (2½ tsp)
Soy sauce (2 tbsp)
Vanilla protein powder (1 scoop)

WEEK 2

Day	Breakfast	Lunch	Dinner	Snack
1	Bacon Wrapped Asparagus	Garlic Rosemary Roasted Chicken Thighs	Asian-style Beef Lettuce Wraps	Apple Slices with Peanut Butter
2	Zucchini and Cheese Hash Browns	Beef and Bell Pepper Skewers	Chicken Fajita Bowl	Chicken Zoodle Soup
3	Chicken Breakfast Patties	Turmeric Ginger Shrimp Stir-fry	Greek Style Chicken Kebabs	Vegan Energy Balls
4	Coconut Flour Pancakes	Ginger Soy Salmon	Thai Coconut Shrimp Curry	Beef and Mushroom Stew
5	Mini Crustless Quiches	Balsamic Glazed Chicken Drumsticks	Grilled Chicken with Roasted Vegetables	Trail Mix
6	Keto Breakfast Burrito Bowl	Herb Infused Lamb Meatballs	Salmon with Lemon Herb Sauce	Spicy Shrimp Coconut Soup
7	Low-Carb Breakfast Pizza	Grilled Chicken and Quinoa Bowl	Beef stir-fry with Broccoli	Cucumber and Hummus Bites

GROCERY LIST

Fruits and Vegetables
Apple (1)
Asparagus (12 spears)
Avocado (½)
Baby spinach (1 cup)
Bell peppers (2)
Broccoli florets (3 cups)
Carrots (as part of 2 cups mixed vegetables)
Cauliflower rice (½ cup)
Cherry tomatoes (½ cup)
Cucumber (1 small)
Garlic cloves (3)
Green beans (1 cup)
Lettuce leaves (6 large)
Mixed vegetables (2 cups)
Mushrooms (1 cup)
Onion (¼ cup)
Red bell pepper (1)
Spinach (¼ cup)
Yellow bell pepper (1)
Zucchini (2)

Proteins
Bacon (6 slices)
Beef broth (1 cup)
Beef Sirloin meat (8 oz)
Beef (grounded - 12 oz)
Beef stew meat (8 oz)
Beef lean strips (8 oz)
Chicken breasts (8)
Chicken broth (3 cup)
Chicken drumsticks (3)
Chicken (grounded - 1 lb)
Chicken thighs (2)
Eggs (10)
Lamb (grounded - 4 oz)
Salmon fillets (3)
Shrimp (16 oz)
Turkey (¼ cup)

Cereal and Starch
Coconut flour (2 tbsp)
Low-carb tortillas (2)
Quinoa (1 cup)
Rolled oats (1 cup)

Dairy
Cheddar cheese (1 cup)
Greek yogurt (¼ cup)
Mozzarella cheese (¼ cup)

Non-Dairy
Almond butter (2 tbsp)
Almond milk (¼ cup)
Coconut milk (1½ cups)
Peanut butter (1 tbsp)

Nuts and Seeds
Almonds (2 tbsp)
Chia seeds (1 tbsp)
Sesame seeds (1 tsp)
Walnuts (2 tbsp)

Herbs, Condiments, Spices, and Oils
Baking powder (¼ tsp)
Balsamic vinegar (1 tbsp)
Cocoa powder (1 tbsp)
Dark chocolate chips (1 tbsp)
Dried cranberries (1 tbsp)
Dijon mustard (½ tsp)
Fajita seasoning (1 tbsp)
Fresh Dill (1 tsp)
Garlic powder (1¾ tsp)
Honey (1½ tsp)
Hummus (2 tbsp)
Lemon juice (2½ tbsp)
Lime juice (1 tbsp)
Maple syrup (2 tbsp)
Olive oil (10 tbsp)
Onion powder (½ tsp)
Oregano (1 tsp)
Paprika (2 tsp)
Parsley (1½ tsp dried)
Red curry paste (1 tbsp)
Red pepper flakes (¼ tsp)
Rosemary (fresh - ½ tsp)
Sesame oil (1 tsp)
Soy sauce (low sodium - 3 tbsp)
Thyme (dried -½ tsp)

WEEK 3

Day	Breakfast	Lunch	Dinner	Snack
1	Protein-Packed Veggie Omelet	Vegan Lentil Salad	Vegan Sweet Potato and Black Bean Chili	Roasted Chickpeas
2	Chicken Breakfast Burrito	Turkey and Avocado Wrap	Lemon Garlic Shrimp and Asparagus	Turkey and Spinach Soup
3	Peanut Butter Banana Oatmeal	Shrimp Stir-Fry	Turkey Meatloaf with Green Beans	Zucchini Chips with Parmesan
4	Greek Yogurt Power Bowl	Grilled Salmon Salad	Vegan Tofu Stir-Fry	Creamy Cauliflower and Chicken Soup
5	Sweet Potato and Egg Breakfast Hash	Vegan Chickpea Curry	Baked Cod with Spinach	Turkey and Guacamole Bites
6	Vegan Chocolate Protein Smoothie Bowl	Chicken and Sweet Potato Bowl	Chicken and Quinoa Stir-Fry	Egg Drop Soup with Spinach
7	High-Protein Pancakes	Vegan Buddha Bowl	Vegan Coconut Curry with Chickpeas	Baked Parmesan Crisps

GROCERY LIST

Fruits and Vegetables
Asparagus (1 bunch)
Avocado (1½)
Banana (2)
Bell peppers (3 cups)
Cherry tomatoes (1¼ cups)
Cucumber (½ cup)
Garlic (minced - 2 tsp)
Ginger (grated - 4 tsp)
Mixed berries (strawberries, blueberries, raspberries - ½ cup)
Mixed greens (4½ cups)
Snap peas (1 cup)
Spinach (7 cups)
Sweet potatoes (4 medium)
Zucchini (1½ medium)

Proteins
Chicken breasts (5 medium)
Chickpeas (canned - 3½ cups)
Cod fillets (2 fillets, 4 oz each)
Deli turkey slices (4 slices)
Eggs (12 large)
Firm tofu (1 block)
Salmon fillets (2 fillets - 4 oz each)
Shrimp (peeled and deveined - 24 oz)
Turkey (grounded - 1½ lb)
Turkey breasts (3 oz)

Cereal and Starch
Cereal granola (2 tbsp)
Quinoa (2 cups cooked)
Rolled oats (1½ cups)
Whole-grain tortillas (2)

Dairy
Cheddar cheese (3 tbsp)
Cottage cheese (½ cup)
Feta cheese (¼ cup)
Parmesan cheese (1¼ cups)

Non-Dairy
Almond milk (unsweetened - 1¾ cups)
Chicken broth (6 cups)
Coconut milk (2 cups)
Greek yogurt (1 cup)
Nuts and Seeds
Almond butter (2 tbsp)
Chia seeds (3 tsp)
Hemp seeds (3 tsp)
Peanut butter (1 tbsp)

Herbs, Condiments, Spices, and Oils
Baking powder (1 tsp)
Balsamic vinegar (1 tbsp)
Black pepper (to taste)
Chili powder (1 tsp)
Cinnamon (¼ tsp)
Curry powder (2 tsp)
Dijon mustard (2 tsp)
Garlic powder (1¾ tsp)
Lemon juice (2 tbsp)
Lemon zest (1 tsp)
Olive oil (2½ tbsp)
Onion powder (1 tsp)
Paprika (1¼ tsp)
Salt (to taste)
Sesame oil (1½ tsp)
Soy sauce (low sodium - 4 tbsp)
Tahini (2 tbsp)
Unsweetened cocoa powder (1 tbsp)
Vegan chocolate protein powder (1 scoop)
Vegetable broth (2 cups)
Vanilla protein powder (1 scoop)

WEEK 4

Day	Breakfast	Lunch	Dinner	Snack
1	Avocado Toast with Eggs	Turkey Meatballs Zoodles	Teriyaki Glazed Salmon with Green Beans	Beef Bone Broth Soup
2	Chia Pudding with Protein Boost	Quinoa Stuffed Bell Peppers	Lemon Garlic Grilled Chicken with Asparagus	Greek Yogurt Parfait with Berries and Nuts
3	Tofu Scramble with Vegetables	Lentil and Kale Soup	Herb-Crusted Cod with Steamed Broccoli	Kale and Sausage Stew
4	Spinach and Feta Omelet	Chicken and Chickpea Salad	Grilled Steak with Chimichurri Sauce	Hard Boiled Eggs with Avocado Slices
5	Spinach and Egg Muffins	Chicken and Spinach Stuffed Bell Peppers	Mediterranean Baked Sardines	Lemon Dill Chicken Soup
6	Turkey and Avocado Breakfast Scramble	Salmon and Avocado Lettuce wrap	Spicy Grilled Tuna Steak	Protein-Packed Smoothie
7	Cheesy Omelet with Spinach and Mushrooms	Eggplant and Chicken Caprese Bake	Teriyaki Glazed Chicken Breast	Creamy Broccoli and Cheddar Soup

GROCERY LIST

Fruits and Vegetables
Arugula (1 cup)
Asparagus spears (1 cup)
Avocados (2)
Banana (1)
Bell peppers (5)
Broccoli (3 cups)
Celery (1 cup)
Cherry tomatoes (¾ cup)
Eggplant (1)
Garlic clove (4)
Green beans (1 cup)
Kale (3 cups)
Lettuce leaves (4 large)
Mixed berries (blueberries and raspberries - ½ cup)
Mushrooms (¼ cup)
Onions (¼ cup)
Spinach (2½ cups)
Strawberries (¼ cup)
Tomatoes (1 cup)
Zucchinis (3)

Proteins
Beef bone broth (2 cups)
Beef (½ cup)
Beef Sirloin steak (8 oz)
Black beans (½ cup)
Chicken breasts (16 oz)
Chicken sausage (2)
Cod fillet (4 oz)
Chickpeas (canned - ½ cup)
Eggs (14)
Firm tofu (4 oz)
Lentils (½ cup)
Salmon fillets (8 oz)
Sardines (4)
Turkey (grounded - 12 oz)
Tuna steak (1)

Cereal and Starch
Quinoa (1 cup, cooked)
Whole-grain bread (1 slice)

Dairy
Cheddar cheese (½ cup)
Feta cheese (1 cup)
Greek yogurt (1 cup)
Heavy cream (¼ cup)
Milk (1 tbsp)
Mozzarella cheese (½ cup)

Non-Dairy
Almond milk (unsweetened - 2½ cups)
Chicken broth (5 cups)

Nuts and Seeds
Almonds or walnuts (chopped - 2 tbsp)
Chia seeds (3 tbsp)
Peanut butter (1 tbsp)

Herbs, Condiments, Spices, and Oils
Black Pepper (to taste)
Chili flakes (to taste)
Coconut aminos (½ tbsp)
Cumin (1 tsp)
Dried oregano (½ tsp)
Dried parsley (½ tsp)
Dried parsley (½ tsp)
Dried thyme (½ tsp)
Fresh dill (1 tbsp)
Fresh parsley (2 tbsp)
Garlic powder (2¼ tsp)
Honey or maple syrup (2 tsp)
Lemon juice (3½ tbsp)
Lime juice (½ tbsp)
Marinara sauce (½ cup)
Olive oil (8 tbsp)
Paprika (1 tsp)
Salt (to taste)
Sesame oil (1½ tsp)
Soy sauce (1 tsp)
Turmeric (¼ tsp)
Vegetable broth (1 cup)
Vanilla protein powder (1½ scoops)

CONCLUSION

We hope that you have learned many new things from this book. Also, you are well acquainted with the benefits of a low-carb, high-protein diet. By switching to this diet, you can improve your general well-being, energy levels, and health. You have the skills, information, and recipes to kickstart this new lifestyle journey. Remember, consistency is the key. Build routines that meet your needs by using meal planning techniques, grocery lists, and recipes as a starting point. Keep an eye on your development and modify recipes to fit your tastes. Honor your accomplishments, no matter how minor, and have faith in the process.

Moreover, do not take the tip for success lightly. These tips are life-saviors and we are 100% sure that these will help you to follow the diet stringently.

The perk of consulting this book is that you can ace your nutritional objectives while savoring tasty meals by combining scrumptious meals, helpful advice, and a p lanned meal schedule.

A low-carb diet might be difficult, especially if you love sweets and grains. Carbs or sweetened foods can instantly perk up your mood. But you have to control your cravings by choosing a smaller food serving. This approach will not leave you craving endlessly for a sweet bite.

The resources in this book will enable you to make wise health choices and make you an organized person who plans meals beforehand. If you follow all the guidelines, then you can make it a sustainable diet that you can follow for a lifetime. Wish you luck that you succeed on your journey to better health. Cheers to more delicious dinners and a healthy you!

REFERENCES

1. High Protein, Low Carb Diet: A Complete Guide [Internet]. [cited 2025 Jan 2]. Available from: https://www.healthline.com/nutrition/high-protein-low-carb-diet#diet-types

2. The Zone Diet: A Complete Overview [Internet]. [cited 2025 Jan 2]. Available from: https://www.healthline.com/nutrition/zone-diet#TOC_TITLE_HDR_5

3. Sugar Busters Diet Plan Review: Food List, How It Works, and More [Internet]. [cited 2025 Jan 3]. Available from: https://www.webmd.com/diet/a-z/sugar-busters-what-it-is

4. Shai I, Schwarzfuchs D, Henkin Y, Shahar DR, Witkow S, Greenberg I, et al. Weight Loss with a Low-Carbohydrate, Mediterranean, or Low-Fat Diet. N Engl J Med. 2008 Jul 17;359(3):229–41.

LOW-CARB, HIGH PROTEIN COOKBOOK.

DELICIOUS & NUTRITIOUS RECIPES FOR A HEALTHIER YOU: FUEL YOUR BODY WITH LOW CARB, HIGH PROTEIN MEALS

This cookbook offers a variety of flavorful low-carb, high-protein recipes thoughtfully designed to support a healthy and balanced lifestyle. With simple instructions and wholesome ingredients, these dishes make it easy to create satisfying meals and treats that align with your nutritional goals.

Perfect for home cooks of all skill levels, this collection will inspire you to explore the possibilities of delicious, health-conscious cooking.

YOUR FEEDBACK IS INVALUABLE—SHARE YOUR REVIEW TO HELP OTHERS ON THEIR JOURNEY TO HEALTHIER, HAPPIER EATING!

RECIPE INDEX

Spinach and Egg Muffins   22
Turkey and Avocado Breakfast Scramble   22
Cheesy Omelet with Spinach and Mushrooms   23
Salmon and Avocado Breakfast Bowl 23
Greek Yogurt and Almond Butter Parfait   24
Sausage and Egg Breakfast Cups   24
Almond Flour Waffles 25
Bacon Wrapped Asparagus   25
Zucchini and Cheese Hash Browns   26
Chicken Breakfast Patties   26
Coconut Flour Pancakes   27
Mini Crustless Quiches   27
Keto Breakfast Burrito Bowl   28
Low- Carb Breakfast Pizza   28
Protein Packed Veggie Omelet 29
Chicken Breakfast Burrito   29
Peanut Butter Banana Oatmeal   30
Greek Yogurt Power Bowl   30
Sweet Potato and Egg Breakfast Hash   31
Vegan Chocolate Protein Smoothie Bowl   31
High- Protein Pancakes   32
Avocado Toast with Eggs   33
Chia Pudding with Protein Boost 33
Tofu Scramble with Vegetables 34
Spinach and Feta Omelet   34
Greek Yogurt Parfait with Berries and Nuts 37
Hard Boiled Eggs with Avocado Slices   37
Protein-Packed Smoothie   38
Veggie sticks with Hummus   38
Cottage Cheese and Pineapple Bowl 39
Rice Cakes with Almond Butter and Banana 39
Tuna Salad with Crackers   40
Apple Slices with Peanut Butter 40
Vegan Energy Balls   41
Trail Mix   41
Cucumber and Hummus Bites   42

Roasted Chickpeas 42
Zucchini Chips with Parmesan 43
Turkey and Guacamole Bites 43
Baked Parmesan Crisps   44
Chicken and Spinach Stuffed Bell Peppers 46
Salmon and Avocado Lettuce Wrap 46
Eggplant and Chicken Caprese Bake 47
Tuna and Cucumber Boats 47
Shrimp and Cauliflower Rice Bowl 48
Grilled Chicken and Asparagus 48
Seared Tofu with Broccoli   49
Garlic Rosemary Roasted Chicken Thighs   49
Beef and Bell Pepper Skewers 50
Turmeric Ginger Shrimp Stir- Fry 50
Ginger Soy Salmon   51
Balsamic Glazed Chicken Drumsticks 51
Herb Infused Lamb Meatballs 52
Grilled Chicken and Quinoa Bowl 52
Vegan Lentil Salad   53
Turkey and Avocado Wrap   54
Shrimp Stir- Fry   54
Grilled Salmon Salad   55
Vegan Chickpea Curry 55
Chicken and Sweet Potato Bowl 56
Vegan Buddha Bowl   57
Turkey Meatballs Zoodles   57
Quinoa Stuffed Bell Peppers   58
Lentil and Kale Soup   58
Chicken and Chickpea Salad   59
Chicken Zoodle Soup 61
Beef and Mushroom Stew   61
Spicy Shrimp Coconut Soup   62
Turkey and Spinach Soup   62
Creamy Cauliflower and Chicken Soup   63
Egg Drop Soup with Spinach 63
Beef Bone Broth Soup 64
Kale and Sausage Stew   64
Lemon Dill Chicken Soup   65
Creamy Broccoli and Cheddar Soup 65

Mediterranean Baked Sardines 67
Spicy Grilled Tuna Steak 67
Teriyaki Glazed Chicken Breast 68
Garlic Butter Shrimp and Zoodles 68
Beef and Vegetable Stir- Fry 69
Pesto chicken with Roasted Brussels Sprouts 69
Cajun Salmon with Cabbage Slaw 70
Asian style Beef Lettuce Wraps 70
Chicken Fajita Bowl 71
Greek Style Chicken Kebabs 71
Thai Coconut Shrimp Curry 72
Grilled Chicken with Roasted Vegetables 72
Salmon with Lemon Herb Sauce 73
Beef stir-fry with Broccoli   73
Vegan Sweet Potato and Black Bean Chili   74
Lemon Garlic Shrimp and Asparagus 74
Turkey Meatloaf with Green Beans 75
Vegan Tofu Stir- Fry   75
Baked Cod with Spinach   76
Chicken and Quinoa Stir- Fry 77
Vegan Coconut Curry with Chickpeas 77
Teriyaki Glazed Salmon with Green Beans   78
Lemon Garlic Grilled Chicken with Asparagus   78
Herb-Crusted Cod with Steamed Broccoli   79
Grilled Steak with Chimichurri Sauce 80

Printed in Great Britain
by Amazon